Collins
My First
Encyclopedia

Contents

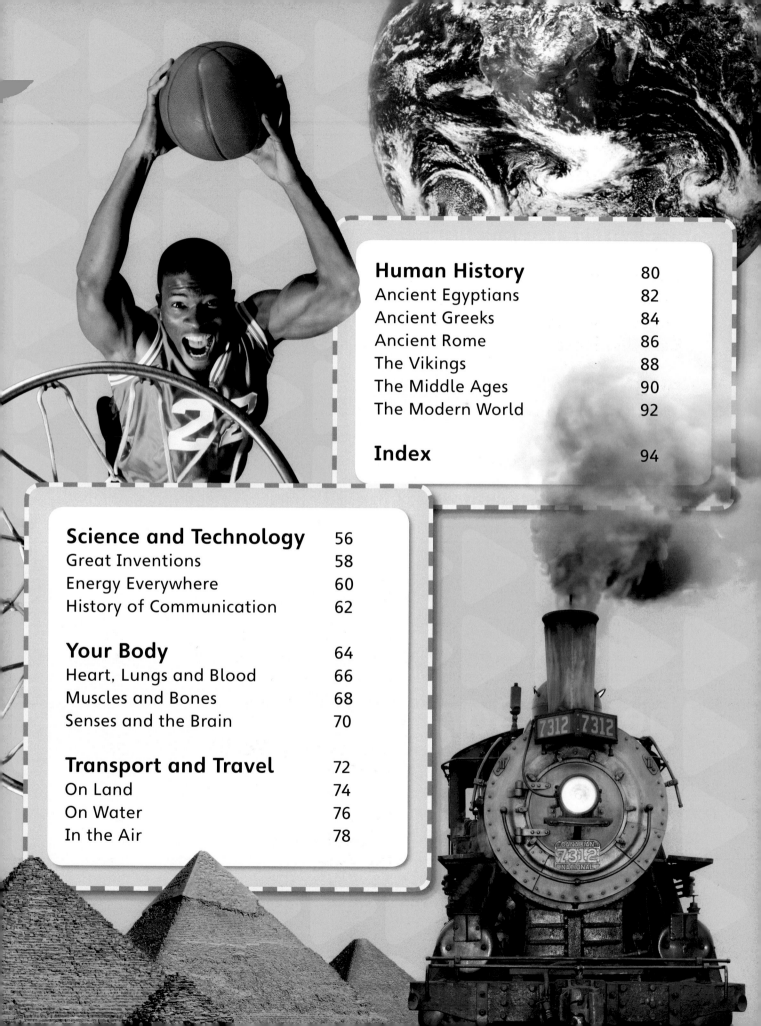

The Universe

Our Earth is surrounded by a vast space called the universe. We are only a tiny part of the universe. The universe is enormous. It contains all of the planets and stars. No one even knows how big the universe is. What we do know is that it's getting bigger every day.

The Big Bang

Scientists think the universe was created by a big explosion about 13.7 billion years ago. Pieces from the explosion spread out and turned into stars and galaxies. This is known as the Big Bang theory. NASA's Spitzer Space Telescope observed a fledgling solar system, like the one depicted in this artist's concept, and discovered deep within it enough water vapour to fill the oceans on the Earth five times.

Galaxies

On a clear night you can see thousands of stars in the sky. They look like twinkling white dots. A group of stars is called a galaxy. There can be billions of stars in one galaxy. The universe has about a hundred billion different galaxies.

Types of Galaxies

A barred spiral galaxy has a spiral shape and a bar of stars at its centre.

A spiral galaxy has a spiral shape, like a pinwheel or a snail's shell.

An irregular galaxy has no real shape. Many were once spiral or elliptical galaxies.

An elliptical galaxy has an oval shape.

Stars

Stars are massive balls of burning gas. They send out heat and light in every direction. Stars may look the same from Earth, but they are all different sizes and temperatures. The closest star to the Earth is the Sun. It is an average-sized star.

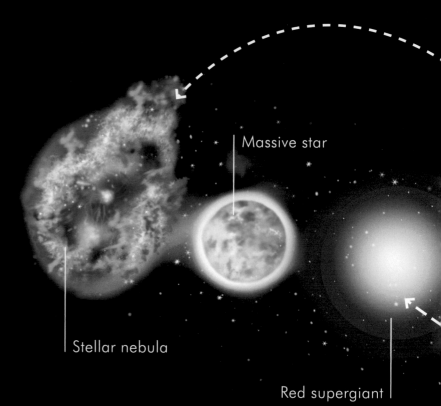

Massive star

Stellar nebula

Red supergiant

Constellations

Some groups of stars look like patterns. They appear in a particular region of the sky. These groups are called constellations. In the past, sailors used stars to guide them on the seas.

Ursa Minor or the Little Bear

The Southern Cross

Life of a Star

A Star's Birth
A star is born in a cloud of gas and dust called a stellar nebula. This shrinks until it becomes a spinning ball of hot gas—a star.

An Adult Star
The star shines steadily for millions of years. Stars which exhaust their energy faster than others have shorter lives.

Supernova

Black hole

Neutron star

Death of a Star
Once a star uses up its energy it starts to die. The star swells up to 100 times its size to become a red supergiant. This may explode into a supernova and then become a black hole or neutron star.

Shooting Stars

Sometimes, burning pieces of dust or rock hurtle towards Earth. These are called shooting stars, but they are actually meteoroids—pieces of matter from space. These pieces burn up when they hit the layer of air around Earth.

◄ **People often make a wish when they see a shooting star.**

Our Solar System

Our solar system is like a city with the Sun at its centre. Eight planets and other objects revolve around it. This is because the Sun has a lot of gravity, a force that pulls objects toward it.

The Sun

is a huge ball of hot gas that holds our solar system together. It is the Sun's energy that keeps all life on Earth alive. Without this energy Earth would be a cold and dark place.

Saturn

has rings around it, with pieces of rock and ice that shine in the sunlight.

Jupiter

is the biggest planet in the solar system and has 63 moons.

Mars

is called the red planet and has icecaps and dust storms.

Earth

is the only planet in the solar system known to have life.

The Moon

The Moon circles around Earth. It is dry and dusty. Its surface has mountains and holes called craters.

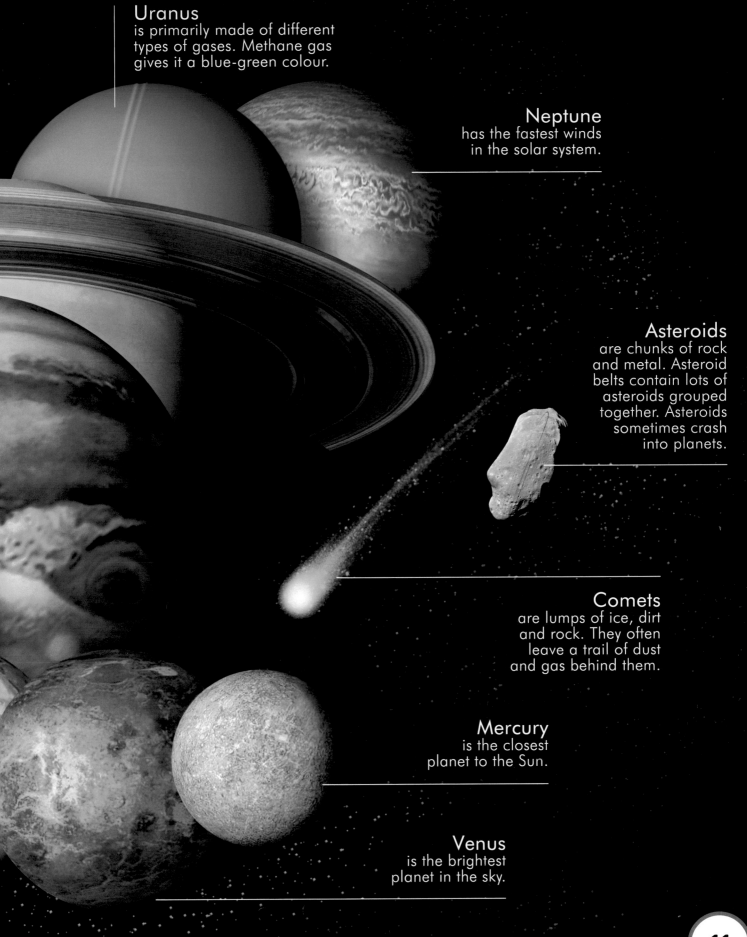

Uranus
is primarily made of different
types of gases. Methane gas
gives it a blue-green colour.

Neptune
has the fastest winds
in the solar system.

Asteroids
are chunks of rock
and metal. Asteroid
belts contain lots of
asteroids grouped
together. Asteroids
sometimes crash
into planets.

Comets
are lumps of ice, dirt
and rock. They often
leave a trail of dust
and gas behind them.

Mercury
is the closest
planet to the Sun.

Venus
is the brightest
planet in the sky.

Exploring Space

Humans have studied the skies through telescopes for centuries. Today, we can send people to explore space. Space is a dangerous place. That is why probes and rovers are sent out in space. These machines are controlled by computers.

Astronauts

Astronauts are trained to travel into space. They usually stay inside the safety of a spacecraft but sometimes go out into space. They wear special spacesuits to protect themselves.

Eating in Space

Dried food in packets is mixed with water. The water makes the food moist and helps it stick to the spoon.

Drinking in Space

In space, liquid turns into balls and floats away. Astronauts have to drink through straws from packets.

Living in Space

Astronauts live in space on board spacecraft or space stations. But in space everything is weightless. This means astronauts need to stop themselves floating around. It also makes it hard to eat, drink and sleep.

Sleeping in Space

Astronauts often sleep inside sleeping bags tied to the wall. Sometimes they sleep strapped into chairs.

Communications antenna

Solar array

The Hubble Space Telescope

The Hubble Telescope circles the Earth in space. Here, it takes pictures of the universe. It can see galaxies nobody on Earth has ever seen before.

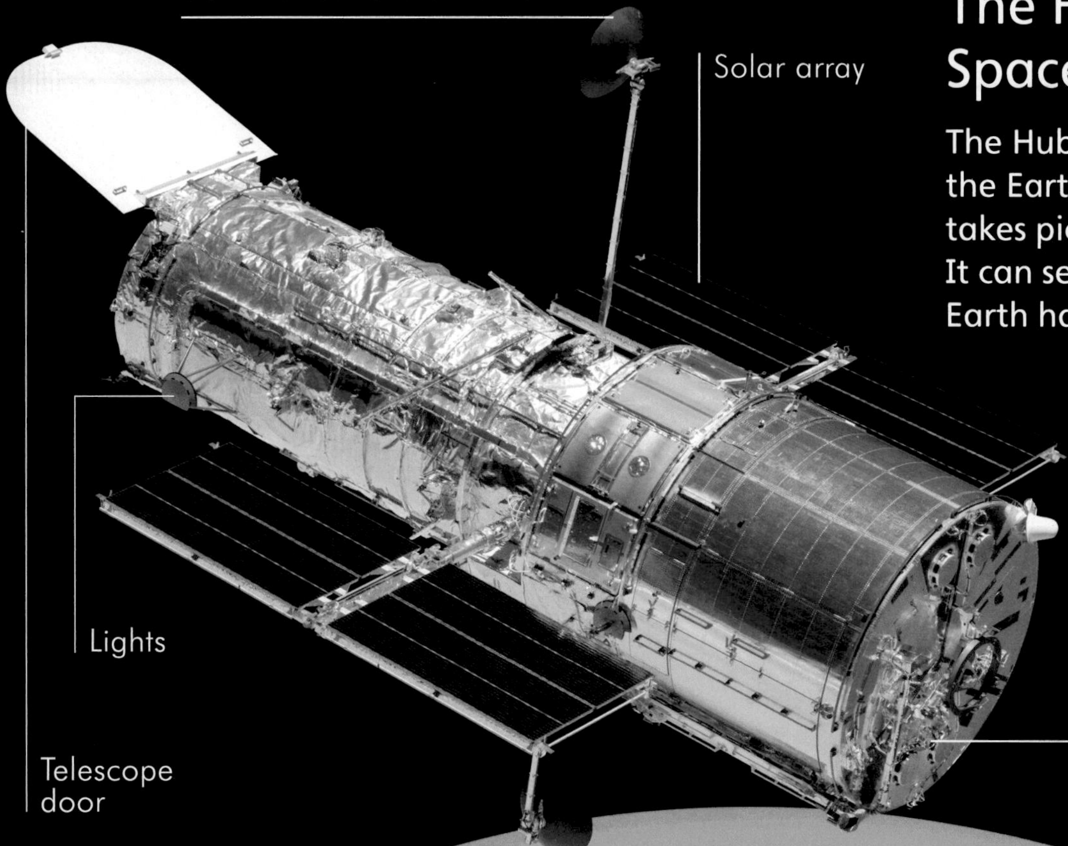

◄ Hubble is powered by energy from the Sun. It takes pictures like a camera and sends them to computers on Earth.

Lights

Telescope door

Mirrors and equipment inside

Space Shuttles

Space shuttles carry astronauts into space. Shuttles can be used over and over again.

◄ Rockets blast space shuttles into space.

USA

13

Earth

Our planet is called Earth. It is the only planet that we know has life on it. This is because it is the perfect distance from the sun. If the Earth were any further away from the Sun we would all freeze. If it were any closer we would all boil.

Space shuttles travel into the thermosphere.

Meteoroids travel to the stratosphere.

Hot-air balloons stay within the troposphere.

Inside the Earth

From space, Earth looks like a blue ball covered in swirling clouds. Inside there are layers of hot rock and metal.

The Crust is a thin layer of solid rock.

The Mantle is made of very hot and solid rocks.

The Inner Core is a solid ball composed almost entirely of iron.

The Outer Core is made of extremely hot liquid lava.

Thermosphere

Mesosphere

Stratosphere

Troposphere

Atmosphere

The atmosphere is a layer of invisible gases around the Earth. It protects all life on Earth. It contains the oxygen that we breathe. It stops us from burning in the Sun's rays. It also keeps the Earth's surface at the right temperature.

Aeroplanes, like meteoroids, travel to the stratosphere.

Spinning Earth

All planets travel around the Sun. Earth takes a little over 365 days to travel around the Sun. Earth moves in another way as well. It spins like a top. It takes 24 hours for it to spin completely around. As Earth spins away from the Sun, day turns to night.

This side of the Earth is facing away from the Sun. It is night time here.

This side of the Earth is facing the Sun. It is daytime here.

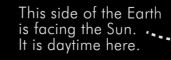

Earth's Landmarks

The Earth is constantly changing the way it looks. Landforms like sand dunes, mountains and valleys dot the Earth's surface. Often these are formed slowly by wind and water. But landforms can also be created suddenly by volcanoes, storms and earthquakes.

Mountains

Mountains are formed when pieces of rock under the ground push against each other. This causes some of the rock to break through the surface and rise up. Mountains usually have a sharp point at the top called a peak.

Glaciers

A glacier is a large river of ice that moves slowly across the land. Glaciers only form in the coldest parts of the world. As a glacier moves it wears down the land beneath it. This causes a large hollow called a valley.

▼ The Pasterze Glacier is 8 km long. It is the largest of Austria's 925 glaciers.

Valleys

A valley is a long hollow in the Earth's surface. Often, valleys have a V or U shape, with steep slopes on either side. Valleys are usually created by rivers or glaciers, which wear away the rock over time.

The Grand Canyon is one of the most ▶ famous valleys in the world. It is 445 km long and is located in America.

Caves

A cave is a hole in the side of a hill, or an underground chamber that opens to the outside world. Most caves are formed by water slowly over time. Usually, water drips through the ground into the soft rock below. This wears the rock down. Eventually this forms an underground cave.

Dunes

A dune is a sand hill found in the desert or at the beach. Dunes are created by the wind and come in many shapes and sizes. Large areas of desert dunes are called ergs. Very few plants grow on dunes.

Dunes don't stay in the ▶ same place forever. Over time, the wind moves them in a particular direction.

17

Oceans and Seas

The Earth is often called the blue planet. This is because seas and oceans cover two-thirds of its surface. There are five main oceans—the Pacific, the Atlantic, the Indian Ocean, the Southern Ocean and the Arctic Ocean.

Fresh or Salty?

The water found in the sea is salty. Humans can only drink freshwater that contains no salt. Only 2.5 percent of the world's water is freshwater. Most of this freshwater is frozen in icebergs or glaciers.

Abyssal plain

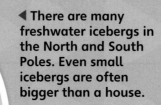

◀ There are many freshwater icebergs in the North and South Poles. Even small icebergs are often bigger than a house.

◀ Humans explore the sea using submarines or diving suits. Air tanks allow people to breathe underwater.

Underwater World

The world under the sea is a mysterious place. There are mountains, valleys and even volcanoes. There are billions of plants and creatures you would never see on land.

How Far to the Bottom?

Oceans are very deep. The Pacific is the deepest ocean. In some places it is over 11,030 metres to the bottom. If the tallest mountain in the world were dropped into the deepest part of this ocean, you would not be able to see the top.

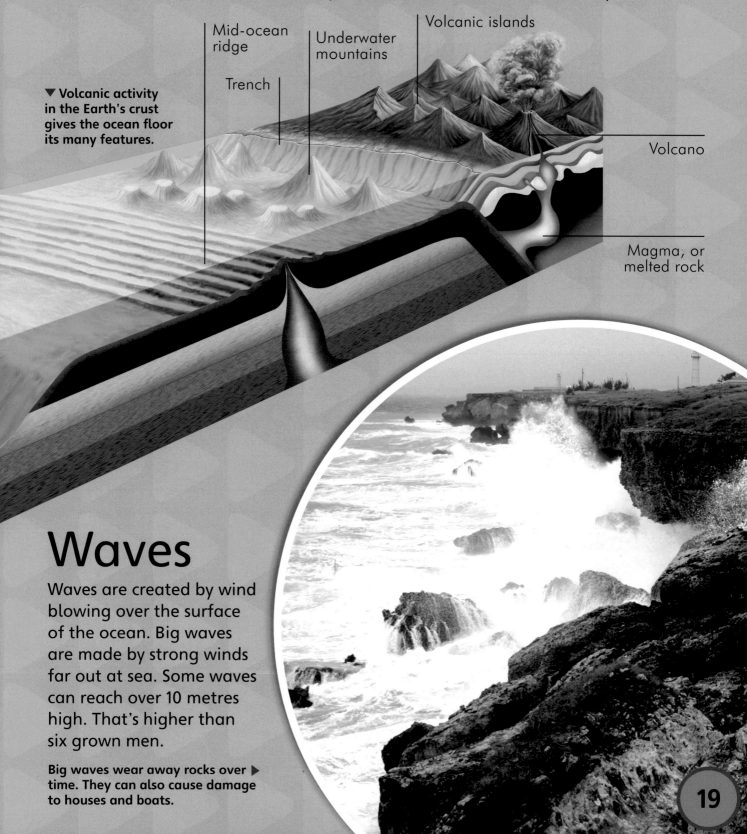

Mid-ocean ridge

Underwater mountains

Volcanic islands

Trench

▼ Volcanic activity in the Earth's crust gives the ocean floor its many features.

Volcano

Magma, or melted rock

Waves

Waves are created by wind blowing over the surface of the ocean. Big waves are made by strong winds far out at sea. Some waves can reach over 10 metres high. That's higher than six grown men.

Big waves wear away rocks over ▶ time. They can also cause damage to houses and boats.

Volcanoes and Earthquakes

The Earth's crust is made up of big pieces of land that fit together like a jigsaw puzzle. These pieces of land are called 'plates'. When two plates bang into each other, it causes an earthquake. Big earthquakes can destroy entire cities.

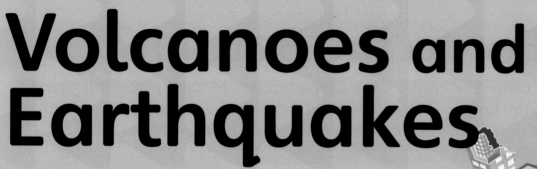

The Earth's crust moves along cracks called fault ▶ lines. Earthquakes normally occur near these cracks.

Earthquakes at Sea

Sometimes earthquakes happen under the sea. This can create a huge wave called a tsunami (below). Some tsunamis reach land. They travel fast and are very high. Big tsunamis often destroy houses and villages.

Volcanoes

A volcano occurs when hot liquid rock erupts through the ground. The hot rock, called lava, spurts into the air and flows down. Ash, dust and chunks of rock are also thrown into the air during an eruption. Volcanoes are often shaped like a cone.

Hot, liquid rock under ▶ the Earth's crust rises up through a hole called a vent.

Burning River

Rivers of lava can flow for many kilometres. They are very dangerous. The lava is so hot it burns anything in its path.

◀ The hotter the lava, the more quickly it flows.

Volcano in Space

The biggest volcano in our solar system isn't on Earth. Olympus Mons on Mars is 27 km high. That's as high as 32 of the Earth's tallest buildings, one on top of another.

Weather

What kind of weather are you having today? Maybe it is sunny, or wet, or windy. There are many different kinds of weather. The sun, water and air are the three things that make weather. The sun brings warmth. The air brings wind. Water brings rain and snow.

The Water Cycle

The Earth does not create new water. Instead it moves water around. Water goes from the oceans, to the air, to the rivers, and back to the oceans. This is called the water cycle.

The water becomes vapour and rises into the sky. There, it cools and becomes water droplets.

The water droplets become clouds.

Water is stored as ice and snow in mountains.

Water falls from the clouds as rain.

Water from the sea evaporates in the sunshine.

Rivers run into the sea.

The rain runs into streams and rivers.

Storms

Storms bring extreme types of weather. They form inside massive clouds that release huge amounts of energy—as much as a nuclear bomb blast. The result can be very fast winds, bolts of lightning and claps of thunder. Storms can destroy towns and villages.

▲ **Floods:** Sometimes a lot of rain can cause rivers to spill over. This causes a flood. The water rushes onto dry land, often ruining things in its path.

▲ **Lightning:** Lightning is a flash of electricity in the sky. A noise called thunder follows lightning.

▲ **Tornado:** A tornado is a spinning tube of wind. It sucks up anything that gets in its way.

▲ **Snow:** Snowflakes fall when the weather is very cold. Every snowflake has a different pattern.

Four Seasons

In most places on Earth there are four seasons. They are spring, summer, autumn and winter. Each new season brings changes in the weather and the temperature. Animals and plants change with the seasons too.

▲ **Spring:** Everything comes to life in spring. Trees grow new leaves and plants blossom. Many animals give birth to their young. The weather becomes warmer.

▲ **Summer:** Things heat up in summer. The trees are green with leaves and the plants grow flowers. Many types of fruit become ripe and ready to eat. The days are long and warm.

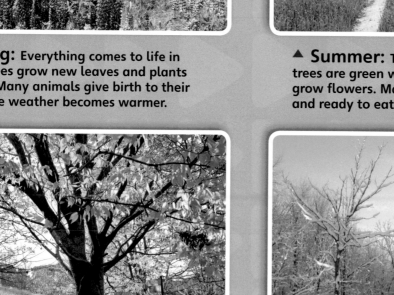

▲ **Autumn:** The days become shorter in autumn and the weather cools down. Trees begin to lose their leaves. Thicker fur starts growing on some animals. Some birds fly to warmer countries.

▲ **Winter:** Winter brings freezing winds, and sometimes snow and rain. Trees are bare and plants stop growing. The days are shorter. Many animals go to sleep for the winter.

North and South

The world has two halves, the north and the south. The halves are called hemispheres. When the north has its summer, the south has its winter. North America, Europe, most of Asia and Africa and a small part of South America are in the northern hemisphere.

Northern hemisphere

Equator

Southern hemisphere

Why are there Seasons?

It takes the Earth one year to travel around the Sun. But the Earth is slightly tilted. This means either the north or the south is closer to the Sun. It changes as the year goes on. This is why our seasons change at different times of the year.

In September neither hemisphere is warmer. It is spring in the south and autumn in the north.

In December the south has summer. The north has winter.

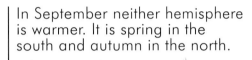

Sun

In June the north has summer. The south has winter.

In March neither hemisphere is warmer. It is spring in the north and autumn in the south.

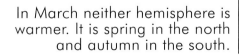

Our World

Most of the Earth's surface is covered by water. Only one-third of Earth is land. This land is broken up into seven continents—Africa, Antarctica, Asia, Australia, Europe, North America and South America. There are many countries in most continents.

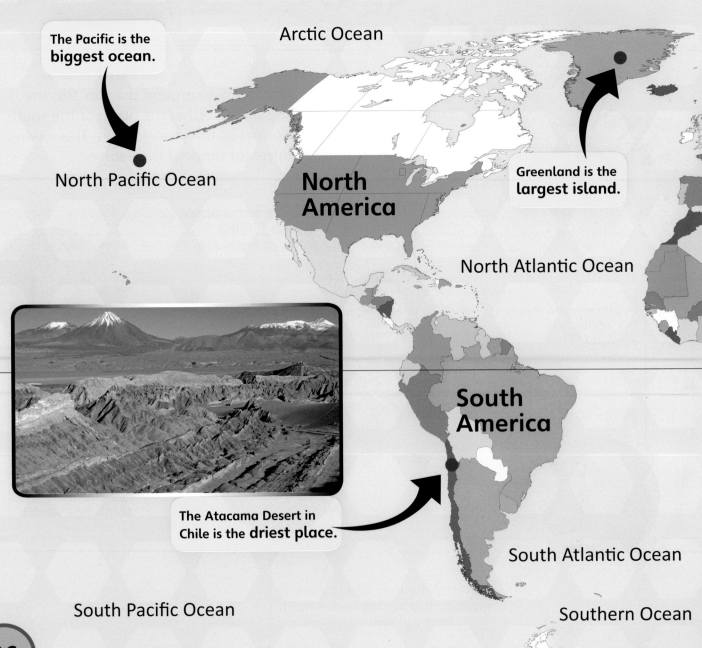

Arctic Ocean

The Pacific is the **biggest ocean.**

North Pacific Ocean

North America

Greenland is the **largest island.**

North Atlantic Ocean

The Atacama Desert in Chile is the **driest place.**

South America

South Atlantic Ocean

South Pacific Ocean

Southern Ocean

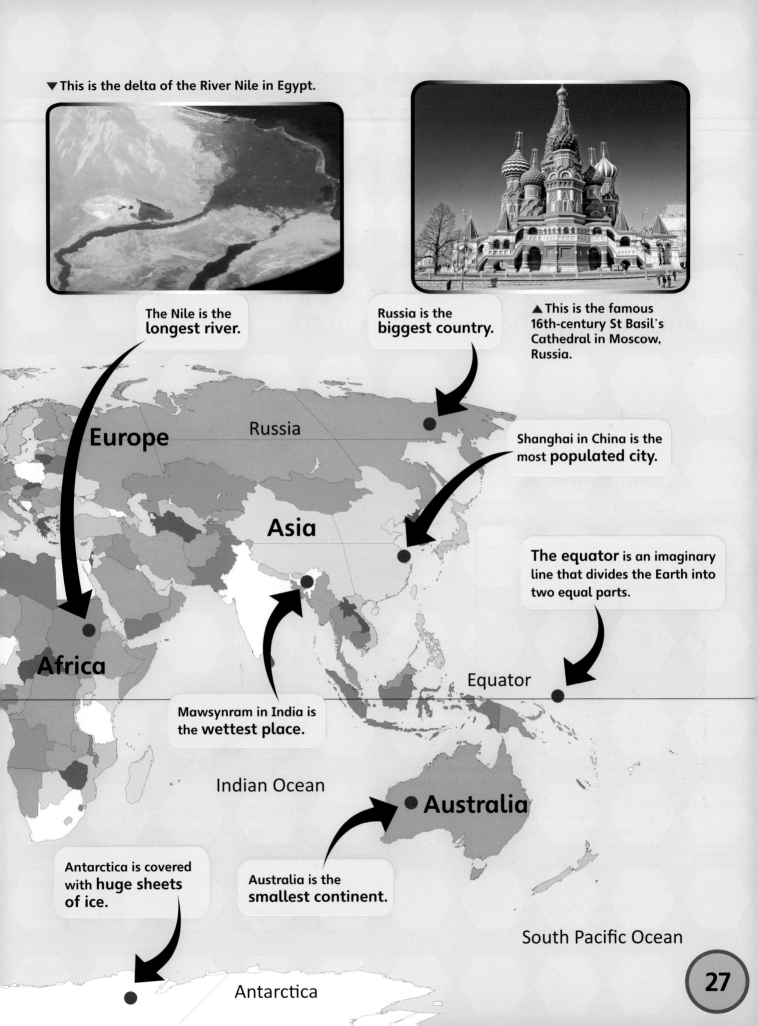

▼ This is the delta of the River Nile in Egypt.

The Nile is the **longest river.**

Russia is the **biggest country.**

▲ This is the famous 16th-century St Basil's Cathedral in Moscow, Russia.

Shanghai in China is the most **populated city.**

Europe

Russia

Asia

The equator is an imaginary line that divides the Earth into two equal parts.

Africa

Equator

Mawsynram in India is the **wettest place.**

Indian Ocean

Australia

Antarctica is covered with **huge sheets of ice.**

Australia is the **smallest continent.**

South Pacific Ocean

Antarctica

Countries of the World

A country is a bordered area of land where people live together. Every country has its own government or leaders. Most countries have their own language and currency. There are 196 countries in the world.

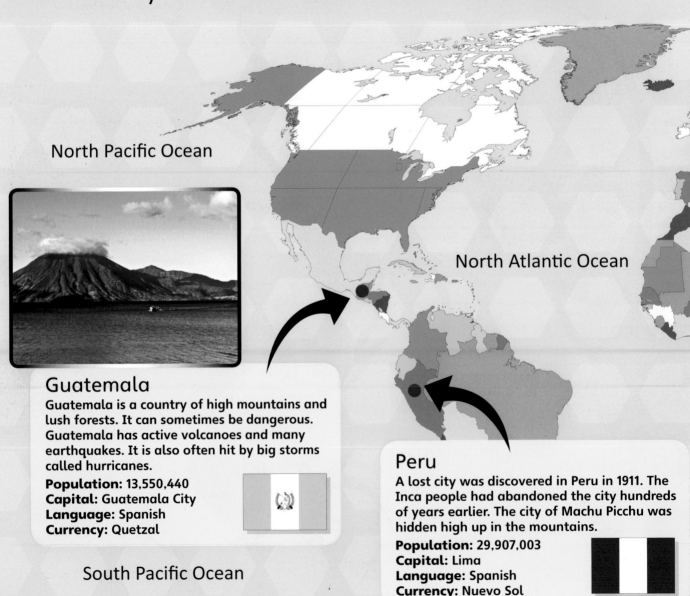

North Pacific Ocean

North Atlantic Ocean

Guatemala
Guatemala is a country of high mountains and lush forests. It can sometimes be dangerous. Guatemala has active volcanoes and many earthquakes. It is also often hit by big storms called hurricanes.

Population: 13,550,440
Capital: Guatemala City
Language: Spanish
Currency: Quetzal

Peru
A lost city was discovered in Peru in 1911. The Inca people had abandoned the city hundreds of years earlier. The city of Machu Picchu was hidden high up in the mountains.

Population: 29,907,003
Capital: Lima
Language: Spanish
Currency: Nuevo Sol

South Pacific Ocean

Southern Ocean

Poland

Poland is famous for its architecture and history. It has an underground church carved completely out of salt. The church, halls and tunnels were all created by miners in an old salt mine.

Population: 38,463,689
Capital: Warsaw
Language: Polish
Currency: Zloty

Mongolia

Many Mongolians travel around the country with herds of their animals. These include goats, yaks, camels, sheep and cows. They live in big tents called gers and get around on horseback.

Population: 3,086,918
Capital: Ulan Bator
Language: Mongolian
Currency: Togrog

Arctic Ocean

Russia

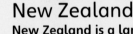

New Zealand

New Zealand is a land where people love sports like rugby, cricket and sailing. It has many forests, lakes, beaches and mountains. It is also full of sheep. There are 10 sheep for every person living there.

Population: 4,369,790
Capital: Wellington
Language: English, Maori
Currency: New Zealand dollar

Indian Ocean

Australia

Tanzania

Tanzania has the highest mountain in Africa. It is also home to many national parks and thousands of animals. These include leopards, zebras, bats, monkeys and elephants.

Population: 41,892,895
Capital: Dodoma
Language: Swahili, English
Currency: Tanzanian shilling

South Pacific Ocean

Antarctica

* Population figures accurate as of 2010.

People of the World

There are over seven billion people living in the world. Every one of them is different. People believe in different things, eat different foods and speak different languages. But people also have many things in common.

A houseboat is a home that ▶ can float on water. These boats are designed so that people can live on board for a long time.

Home

Home is where we eat, sleep, relax and spend time with family. People live in different types of homes. Some sleep in small mud huts. Others live in tall skyscrapers. Some people live on houseboats or in tents.

Clothes and Fashion

People wear clothes to keep warm or stay cool. Others wear a uniform to work or school. Many people wear fashionable clothes they think look good.

◀ Some people, like these girls of China's Zhuang and Dong communities, still wear the traditional clothes of their country.

Sports and Games

People play sport to compete, to keep fit or just for fun. There are lots of popular team sports, such as football and basketball. Other people enjoy games that you can play sitting down, like chess, computer games and cards.

Basketball is one of ▲ the most popular team sports in the world.

Different people ▶ have different skin colours, depending on where their ancestors came from.

31

Religions of the World

Groups of people who believe in a god are religious. Religious people think a god controls what happens on Earth. They often worship their god in a church or temple. There are six main religions in the world.

Christianity

Christians go to church to worship one God and his son Jesus Christ. They believe Jesus came to Earth around 2,000 years ago to teach people about God. The teachings of God are written in a book called the Bible.

Sikhism

Sikhs follow the teachings of a man called Guru Nanak. They worship one God. Sikhs believe in living honest lives and treating everyone equally. Sikhs never cut their hair. Men tie their hair up under a turban.

Hinduism

Hindus worship many gods. The three main gods are Vishnu, Shiva and Brahma. Hindus believe that when a person dies they will be reborn as a different person or animal. A Hindu place of worship is called a temple.

Hindus believe ▼ cows are holy. Hindu temples often feature one or more statues of a cow.

Islam

People who believe in the religion of Islam are called Muslims. They worship a God called Allah in a building called a mosque. When Muslims pray they must face in the direction of Mecca, which is where a prophet called Mohammed was born.

▲ The Kaaba is a shrine in Mecca. Thousands of Muslim pilgrims visit it every year.

Buddhism

Buddhists follow the teachings of a man called Buddha. They believe in peace and harmony. Buddhists worship Buddha in their homes or temples.

◀ Buddhist monks often wear orange or yellow robes. They burn incense while praying.

Judaism

Jewish people follow the religion of Judaism. They read about the laws of God in a book called the Torah. They worship in a synagogue.

The Bar Mitzvah is a Jewish ▶ ceremony that takes place when a boy turns 13. He is then recognised as an 'adult.'

Wonders of the World

People have built many amazing structures throughout history. These include temples, towers and even tombs. Some of the most famous structures are called 'wonders.' They are wonders because they are big, beautiful and were hard to construct.

Petra

Petra is an ancient city in Jordan. It is carved into desert cliffs. Hidden among the rocks, Petra was dry and hot. Special tunnels were constructed to bring water into the city.

Great Wall of China

The Great Wall of China is the longest structure ever built by humans. The wall stretches for 7,300 kilometres. It crosses mountains, valleys and deserts. It was built to protect China from its enemies.

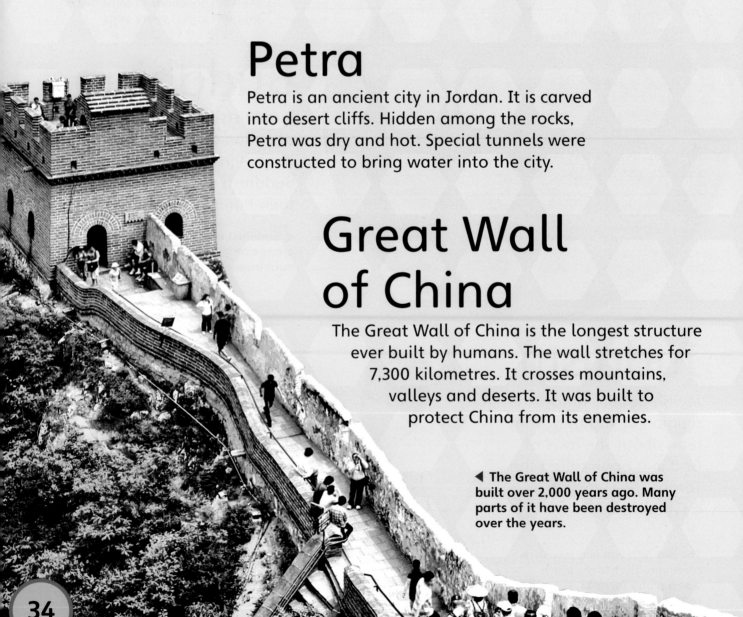

◀ The Great Wall of China was built over 2,000 years ago. Many parts of it have been destroyed over the years.

Taj Mahal

The Taj Mahal is a dazzling white marble building in India. Started in 1632, it took 20,000 workers about 21 years to finish the building.

▲ The emperor Shah Jahan built the Taj Mahal as a tomb for his wife.

Leaning Tower of Pisa

It took about 177 years to build the Tower of Pisa in Italy, but it still wasn't perfect. When it was finished, it started to sink. This made it lean to one side.

Stonehenge

Stonehenge is a circle of huge stones erected thousands of years ago in England. The stones were dragged from hundreds of kilometres away. Some of the stones weigh as much as four elephants. Stonehenge may have been used for rituals and ceremonies, but nobody knows for sure.

Great Pyramid of Giza

The Great Pyramid in Egypt is the largest stone structure ever built. It was constructed over 4,500 years ago as a tomb for Pharaoh Khufu. It took 20,000 men 20 years to complete the pyramid.

The massive limestone blocks and ▶ other materials for the pyramid were brought from quarries across Egypt.

Flags of the World

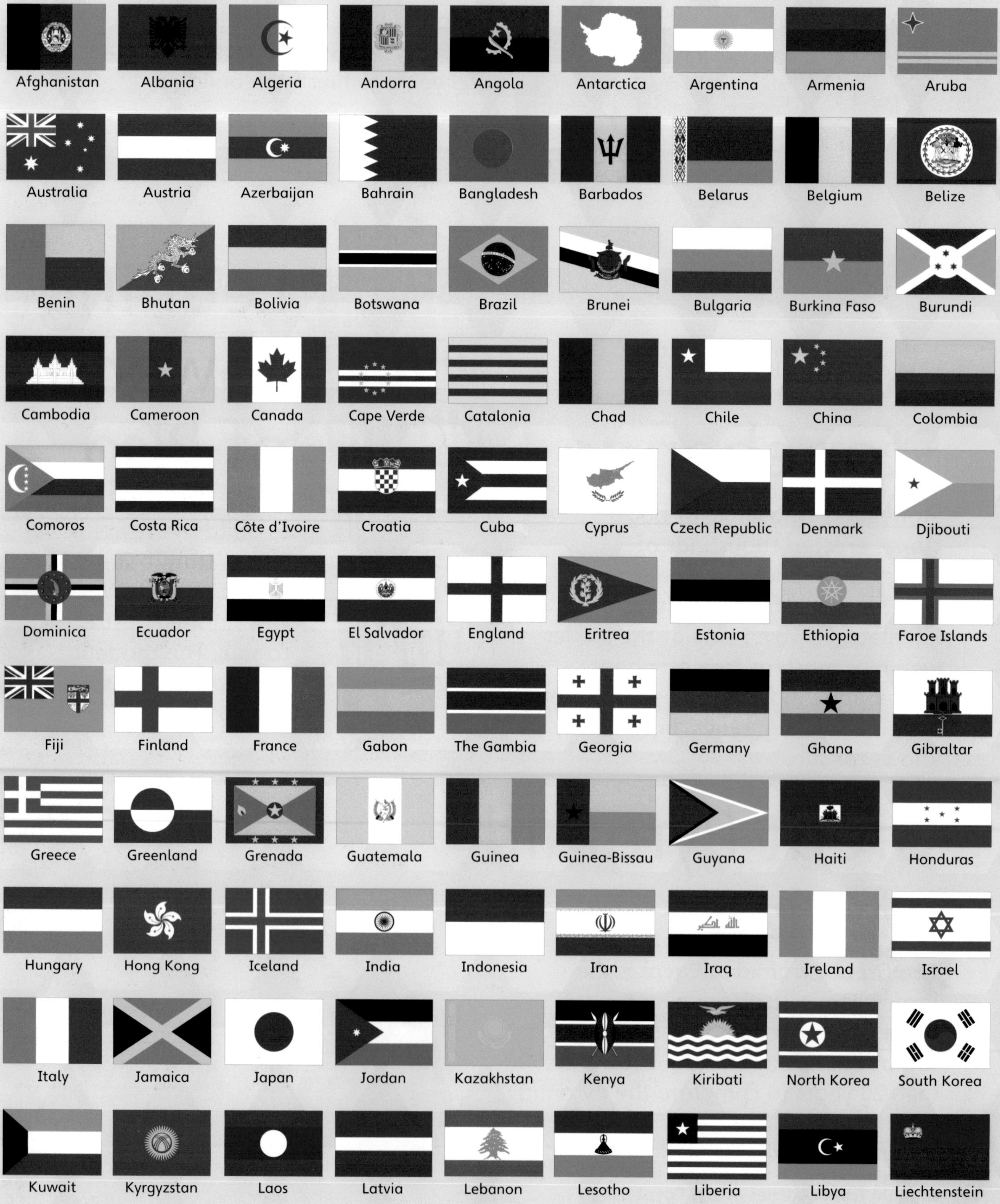

Afghanistan
Albania
Algeria
Andorra
Angola
Antarctica
Argentina
Armenia
Aruba
Australia
Austria
Azerbaijan
Bahrain
Bangladesh
Barbados
Belarus
Belgium
Belize
Benin
Bhutan
Bolivia
Botswana
Brazil
Brunei
Bulgaria
Burkina Faso
Burundi
Cambodia
Cameroon
Canada
Cape Verde
Catalonia
Chad
Chile
China
Colombia
Comoros
Costa Rica
Côte d'Ivoire
Croatia
Cuba
Cyprus
Czech Republic
Denmark
Djibouti
Dominica
Ecuador
Egypt
El Salvador
England
Eritrea
Estonia
Ethiopia
Faroe Islands
Fiji
Finland
France
Gabon
The Gambia
Georgia
Germany
Ghana
Gibraltar
Greece
Greenland
Grenada
Guatemala
Guinea
Guinea-Bissau
Guyana
Haiti
Honduras
Hungary
Hong Kong
Iceland
India
Indonesia
Iran
Iraq
Ireland
Israel
Italy
Jamaica
Japan
Jordan
Kazakhstan
Kenya
Kiribati
North Korea
South Korea
Kuwait
Kyrgyzstan
Laos
Latvia
Lebanon
Lesotho
Liberia
Libya
Liechtenstein

There are 196 countries in the world.
Every country has its own flag.

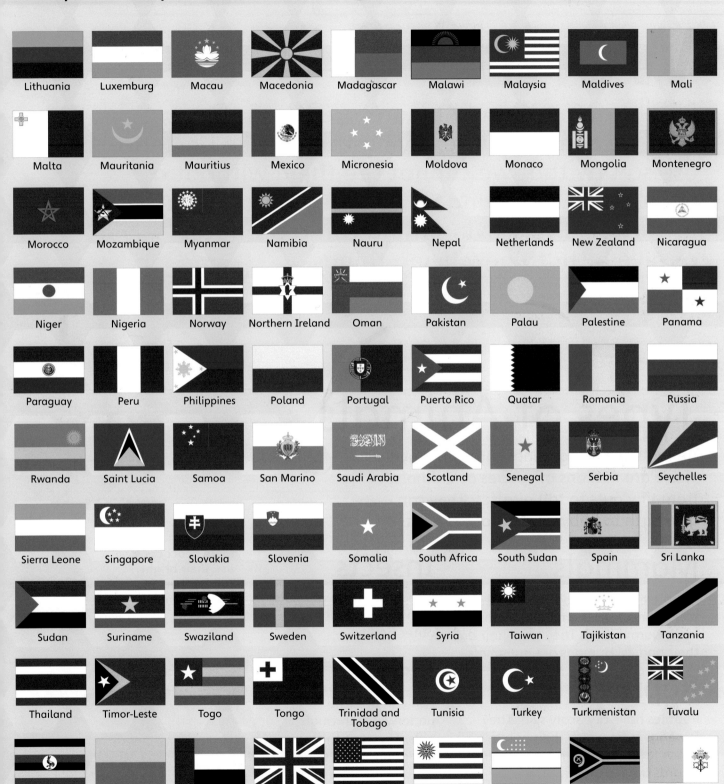

Lithuania | Luxemburg | Macau | Macedonia | Madagascar | Malawi | Malaysia | Maldives | Mali

Malta | Mauritania | Mauritius | Mexico | Micronesia | Moldova | Monaco | Mongolia | Montenegro

Morocco | Mozambique | Myanmar | Namibia | Nauru | Nepal | Netherlands | New Zealand | Nicaragua

Niger | Nigeria | Norway | Northern Ireland | Oman | Pakistan | Palau | Palestine | Panama

Paraguay | Peru | Philippines | Poland | Portugal | Puerto Rico | Quatar | Romania | Russia

Rwanda | Saint Lucia | Samoa | San Marino | Saudi Arabia | Scotland | Senegal | Serbia | Seychelles

Sierra Leone | Singapore | Slovakia | Slovenia | Somalia | South Africa | South Sudan | Spain | Sri Lanka

Sudan | Suriname | Swaziland | Sweden | Switzerland | Syria | Taiwan | Tajikistan | Tanzania

Thailand | Timor-Leste | Togo | Tongo | Trinidad and Tobago | Tunisia | Turkey | Turkmenistan | Tuvalu

Uganda | Ukraine | United Arab Emirates | United Kingdom | United States of America | Uruguay | Uzbekistan | Vanuatu | Vatican City

Venezuela | Vietnam | Wales | Western Sahara | Yemen | Zambia | Zimbabwe

37

Our Living World

Crocodiles are meat-eating ▶ reptiles that live on both land and in water.

Plants, animals and humans are living things that we can see. Other living things, like bacteria, are so tiny that we cannot see them without a microscope. All living things need air and water to survive. Every living thing can reproduce, or give birth to new living things.

Types of Animals

Animals are living things that can move. There are millions of species of animals, from tiny ants to tall giraffes. They can give birth to baby animals or lay eggs.

Animals

Mammals

Female mammals give birth to their young and feed them milk. Mammals have warm blood. They have hair on their bodies. Humans are mammals.

Reptiles

Reptiles have dry, scaly skin. They lay eggs from which their babies hatch later. Reptiles have no hair. Lizards are reptiles.

Insects

Insects are little animals with six legs and hard outer bodies.

Fish

Fish can breathe underwater through gills. They use their fins and tails to swim.

Birds

Birds have feathers and wings. They lay eggs. Almost all birds can fly.

Male peacocks ▼ use their bright tail feathers to attract females.

- Flowering plants produce flowers, seeds and sometimes fruit.
- Mosses live in damp, shady places and have no roots.
- Vines have long stems and grow around other things for support.
- Grasses have narrow leaves and grow close to the ground.

Plants

Plants cannot move around like animals can. Instead they stay in one place and make their own food. They make this food using the sun's energy, water from the soil and gas from the air. Plants contain seeds, which can grow into baby plants.

Trees

Trees are large plants that can live for hundreds of years. They have a thick stem called a trunk and roots that go deep into the ground. These prevent the tree from getting blown away by the wind. Sequoia trees are the largest living things on Earth.

The Sun's energy is caught by the leaves.

The stem supports the plant.

The roots collect water from the ground.

▲ The process by which plants make their food is called photosynthesis. 'Photo' means light and 'synthesis' means to bring together.

Trees help us by ▶ replacing carbon dioxide in the air with oxygen.

Rainforests

Rainforests are hot, wet and bursting with life. Over half the world's species of animals and plants live in them. The Amazon rainforest in South America is the most famous rainforest.

Rainforest Layers

A rainforest has many different layers. These layers begin from the forest floor and end on treetops. Many different plants and creatures live at each layer.

Jaguars

Jaguars are fearsome hunters that eat 85 different species of animals. They often lie across a branch and scoop fish out of the water with their paws.

▼ All jaguars have a unique pattern of spots on their fur.

Emergent trees
Tall trees that tower over other treetops. Eagles and butterflies can be found here.

Canopy
The thick treetops are home to toucans, sloths, monkeys and many other animals.

Sloth
Sloths do almost everything hanging upside down from a branch, including eating and sleeping. Sloths sleep for around 15 hours during the day and wake up to eat leaves at night.

Tarantulas
Tarantulas have large hairy bodies, strong jaws and a deadly bite. They eat insects, lizards, birds and small snakes. They grab their prey with their venomous fangs.

Forest floor
Few plants grow here but it is buzzing with insects and animals like tapirs and gorillas.

A green anaconda can ▶ be up to 6 metres long, as much as three tall men.

Understory
The small trees, shrubs and vines host hummingbirds, snakes, lizards and small mammals.

Anacondas
Anacondas are the largest snakes in the world. They hunt at night, squeezing their prey to death and swallowing them whole. They can swallow an animal the size of a deer.

41

Grasslands

Grasslands are open areas covered by grasses and small shrubs. They are found all over the world. Elephants, giraffes and lions live in African grasslands called savannas. Prairies are grasslands in North America.

A giraffe's long neck ▶ helps it spot enemies from a distance.

Elephants

Elephants are the biggest animals on land. They eat leaves and grass. An elephant uses its trunk to smell, pick things up, put food in its mouth and spray water over itself.

The Tallest Animal

Giraffes are the tallest animals in the world. They grow to about 5.5 metres. They have long necks so they can eat leaves growing high up in the trees. Their long legs help them run at a speed of 60 kilometres an hour.

Zebras

Zebras are covered in black and white stripes. Each one has a slightly different pattern. The stripes help zebras recognise each other. But the stripes also confuse animals trying to hunt zebras.

◀ Male lions have a large mane of hair around their head.

A vulture's ▶ bald head and neck helps it to stay clean.

Lions

Lions live in groups called prides. Together, the pride hunts animals, such as zebras and warthogs. When they are not hunting or eating, lions rest. They rest for up to 20 hours a day.

Vultures

Vultures have very good eyesight and can see food from high in the sky. Vultures usually feed on animals killed by other hunters, such as lions. They wait until the lions leave and then eat what is left.

Rhinos

Rhinos have huge bodies, short stumpy legs and a big horn to protect themselves. They keep cool by lying in muddy water. The mud sticks to their skin and protects them against the sun's heat.

◀ Rhinos live in Africa as well as Asia, but very few of them are left.

- Los Llanos is a tropical grassland in Venezuela and Colombia.
- The Great Plains are grasslands that stretch across the USA and Canada.
- The Southeast Australia temperate savanna is a large grassland in Australia.
- The Mongolian-Manchurian steppe reaches across China, Mongolia and Russia.

Deserts

Deserts are dry places where almost no rain falls. Deserts are often very hot during the day and very cold at night. Some deserts are covered with sand. There are few plants and animals in the desert because it is difficult to survive there.

- The Sahara is the world's largest desert. It covers about 10 percent of Africa, and is about three times as big as the American state of Alaska.
- The Gobi Desert covers about 1,300,000 sq km across Mongolia and China. It is a cold desert. The name 'Gobi' comes from the Mongolian word for 'waterless place.'

Camels

Camels can survive for up to two weeks in the desert without eating or drinking. They live on the fat stored in their humps. Camels have very tough stomachs and can eat almost anything, including grass, meat and even bones.

Rattlesnakes

Rattlesnakes hunt animals at night. They can sense a prey by its body heat and smell. These snakes have a rattle in their tails, which warns off large predators. Rattlesnakes continue to grow throughout their lives.

Scorpions

Scorpions existed long before the dinosaurs. Scorpions have eight legs, a hard shell and a sting in their tails to attack prey with. A scorpion's sting is very painful and requires careful treatment.

Cactuses

Cactuses are spiky plants that can survive for long periods without water. They do this by storing water in the stems and leaves. They use their long roots to collect water from deep underground. Sharp spikes on the cactus make it impossible for most animals to eat it.

45

Under the Ocean

The world under the ocean is brimming with amazing life that never leaves the water. There are millions of different plants and animals living in the seas and oceans. Each creature has a special way of surviving beneath the waves.

Great Barrier Reef

The Great Barrier Reef stretches for more than 2,000 kilometres under the sea. The reef is made up of tiny animals called polyps. When polyps die they leave their skeletons behind. New polyps grow on top of the old ones. This means the reef is always getting bigger.

Blue Whales

The blue whale is the largest animal in the world. It can grow up to 25 metres long and weigh over 150 tonnes. That's longer than six cars and heavier than 25 elephants! Blue whales feed on tiny creatures called plankton and krill. A blue whale's whistle is louder than a jumbo jet, making it the loudest creature on Earth.

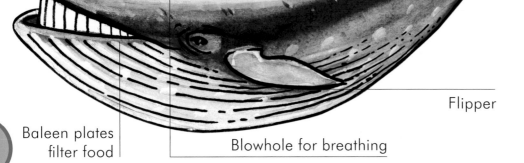

Flukes

Blue-grey skin

Flipper

Baleen plates filter food

Blowhole for breathing

Dolphins

Dolphins are intelligent and playful animals. They live in groups called 'pods' and talk to each other through whistles and clicks. Dolphins cannot breathe underwater, but instead come up to the surface to take in air.

Anglerfish

Anglerfish live in the bottom of the ocean where it is pitch black. Each anglerfish has a special light that hangs like a lantern over its mouth. When other fish come up close to look at the light, the anglerfish gobbles them up. It can swallow a fish over twice its own size.

Octopuses

An octopus has eight arms. These arms have suckers that the octopus uses to grab its prey. It hides in cracks in the rock and can change colour to match its surroundings. When an octopus is attacked, it squirts ink at its hunter so it can get away. If an octopus loses an arm it can grow another one in its place.

Sharks

Dorsal fin

With their huge mouths and rows of sharp teeth, sharks were born to hunt. They have powerful jaws and can smell blood from hundreds of metres away. The great white is the largest shark and can grow to over 7 metres long.

Caudal fin

Thousands of teeth are grown and lost in a lifetime.

Pectoral fin

47

The Poles

The poles are frozen places at the top and bottom of the world. The top pole is called the North Pole and the bottom pole is called the South Pole. The land around the poles is covered with ice and temperatures are usually below freezing. Very few animals can survive there.

Polar Bears

Polar bears are the largest bears in the world and are only found in the Arctic. Their thick fur protects them against the cold. Polar bears hunt seals at breathing holes. When the seal comes up to breathe the polar bear grabs it.

▶ Polar bears are the largest meat-eating land animal.

- **Arctic**
  The area around the North Pole is called the Arctic. It is mainly ocean covered with ice. Some of the ice melts in the summer, but freezes again in the winter. In summer, the sun never sets and it is always light.

- **Antarctica**
  Antarctica is a whole continent covered in ice. The ice never melts. In winter, the sea around the land freezes. It is too cold for humans to live in Antarctica. The South Pole is in the middle of Antarctica.

Killer Whales

Killer whales, or orcas, are the great hunters of the sea. They live together in groups called 'pods.' The members of a pod will hunt together, sometimes attacking very big whales. They will also grab seals from very shallow water.

Penguins

Penguins are black and white birds that cannot fly. Their wings are modified flippers used for swimming and leaping out of water. After a female penguin lays eggs, she leaves to look for food. The male looks after the eggs in the meantime. Most penguins live in Antarctica. You will never find them near the Arctic.

▼ Penguins come to land only to breed or have babies. They live in big groups, called colonies.

Weddell Seals

Weddell seals live close to the South Pole and have short, thick fur. Their short, dense fur keeps them warm in the icy cold Antarctic.

Arctic Terns

The Arctic tern travels farther than any other bird in the world. It spends one summer in the Arctic and then flies to Antarctica for the summer. Every year it flies more than 70,000 kilometres, that is like flying around Earth twice.

Walruses

Walruses are huge Arctic animals with thick brown skin. Males have long tusks. Walruses are slow and clumsy on land, but are very good swimmers. A walrus uses its tusks to pull itself out of the water and to break holes in the ice.

A World of Birds

Birds are animals with feathers and wings. Most birds can fly. They have hollow bones to make them light, and strong wings to lift them. There are over 10,000 different species, or types, of birds in the world, from the tiny hummingbird to the gigantic ostrich.

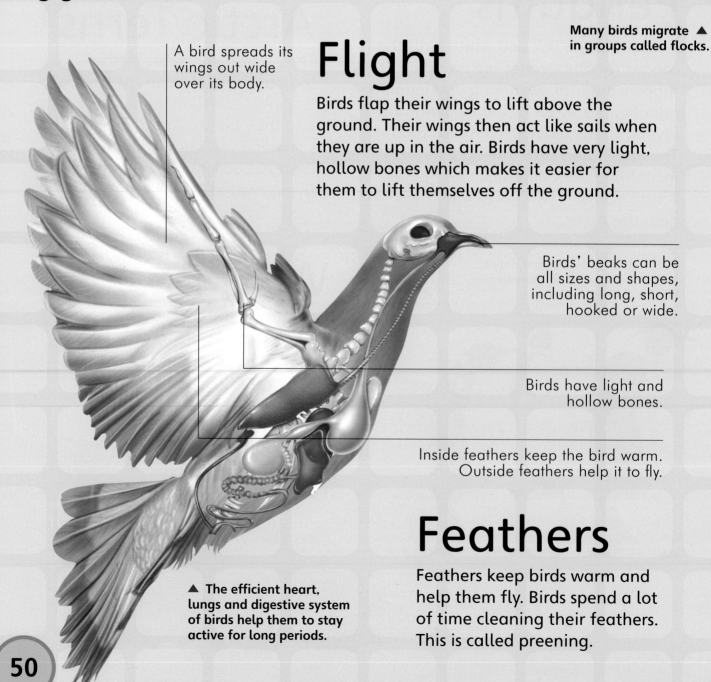

Many birds migrate ▲ in groups called flocks.

Flight

Birds flap their wings to lift above the ground. Their wings then act like sails when they are up in the air. Birds have very light, hollow bones which makes it easier for them to lift themselves off the ground.

A bird spreads its wings out wide over its body.

Birds' beaks can be all sizes and shapes, including long, short, hooked or wide.

Birds have light and hollow bones.

Inside feathers keep the bird warm. Outside feathers help it to fly.

▲ The efficient heart, lungs and digestive system of birds help them to stay active for long periods.

Feathers

Feathers keep birds warm and help them fly. Birds spend a lot of time cleaning their feathers. This is called preening.

Migration

Birds are great travellers. Many birds fly thousands of kilometres to escape cold weather. Others travel to meet a mate or to find food. This travelling is called migration.

A mother bird ▶ swallows food and then spits it back up to feed her babies.

- **Hummingbird**
  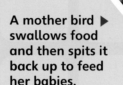
  The hummingbird is the smallest bird in the world. It can beat its wings up to 90 times a second. Hummingbirds can hover in one place and even fly backwards.

- **Non-flyers**
  Not all birds can use their wings. The kiwi is a bird that forgot how to fly. It eats insects and grubs from the ground with its long beak.

- **Birds of Prey**
  Birds of prey are birds that hunt, such as eagles. They have great eyesight and can spot a prey from high up in the sky. They then tuck in their wings and dive towards the ground. They can scoop up their prey in just a few seconds.

- **Ostrich**
  The ostrich is the biggest bird in the world. Its egg weighs 1.5 kilograms (3.3 lb). That's as heavy as 20 chicken eggs. Ostriches cannot fly, but they can run faster than any other bird.

- **Talking Birds**
  Most birds can sing. Some twitter, chirp or tweet. Some parrots can even talk. They do this by copying what a person says. Then they say it over and over again.

Chicks and Nests

A female bird makes a nest and lays her eggs in it. She sits gently on top of the eggs to keep them warm. When the baby is ready to hatch, it breaks through the shell. The young hatchlings have no feathers and keep their eyes shut. The baby birds are always hungry and make a lot of noise, so the parent birds must shuttle back and forth from the nest with food.

▼ Macaws are a large and colourful type of parrot. They are smart and can copy different sounds and words.

A World of Insects

Insects come in many shapes and sizes, but all of them have six legs. They also have a hard outer shell protecting their bodies. Many insects have wings. There are over a million different types of insects.

Ladybird eggs

Laying eggs

Small

Wasp

The smallest insect is a Tanzanian parasitic wasp. It is smaller than a fly's eye. The wasp survives by living inside a larger animal.

◀ **Wasps sting but they kill other harmful insects.**

Interesting Insects

Smart

Ants are very clever. They build huge dirt cities under the ground called colonies. Every ant in a colony has a job, such as worker, soldier or nurse.

◀ **Leafcutter ants cut leaves and grow fungus on these to feed their larvae.**

Scary

The giant weta is one of the heaviest insects in the world. It can weigh more than a sparrow. Giant wetas may look frightening, but they are slow and gentle creatures.

▼ Life cycle of a Ladybird

Larva leaving egg

Larva attaching itself to leaf

Young adult emerging

Adult

Young adult

Mature larva

Mosquito

Butterflies drink ▶ nectar from flowers.

◀ Mosquitoes can transfer germs when they bite.

Harmful or Helpful?

Some insects, like butterflies, help plants grow. They transfer pollens from one plant to another and help in spreading seeds, so new plants can grow. Some other insects, like mosquitoes, are harmful. Mosquitoes spread a disease called malaria, which can kill people.

Dinosaurs

Millions of years ago reptiles ruled the Earth. Some were bloodthirsty meat eaters that generally walked on two legs. Others were gentle plant eaters that walked on four legs. These were the dinosaurs.

T-Rex

The Tyrannosaurus Rex was one of the fiercest dinosaurs. It stood 6 metres high on strong legs with large, clawed feet. It had jagged teeth that were 18 centimetres long. The T-Rex could have swallowed a person whole with its wide jaws.

Big and Small

- The biggest dinosaur was the Giganotosaurus (say 'jig-a-noot-a-saw-rus'). They had sharp and narrow teeth.
- The smallest dinosaur was the Compsognathus (say 'comp-sog-nath-us'). It was the size of a chicken.

◄ The Giganotosaurus was even larger than the T-Rex. It snacked on other large dinosaurs.

Stegosaurus

The Stegosaurus (say 'steg-a-saw-rus') had a line of bony plates on its back to stop attackers jumping on it. The plates would also help the dinosaur warm up in the sun. The Stegosaurus had a deadly spiked tail, which it would swing at attacking meat eaters.

Deinonychus

The Deinonychus (say 'die-non-ee-kuss') was a small, smart and speedy meat-eating dinosaur. It had over 60 razor-sharp teeth and hunted in packs. Deinonychus also had three long claws on each hand to slash its prey with.

A pack of hungry Deinonychus ▶ could kill larger dionosaurs.

Off the Land

Dinosaurs were reptiles that lived on land. There were also flying reptiles and reptiles in the sea.

- The Kronosaurus (say 'krow-no-saw-rus') had four flippers, a short tail and a huge head. It probably ate most things it came across.

- The Pteranodon (say 'ter-an-o-don') was a flying reptile with a long beak and wings made of skin, like a bat.

The End of Dinosaurs

Dinosaurs walked the Earth for over 160 million years. But all of a sudden they disappeared. Scientists think a huge meteorite hit Earth covering it in an ash cloud. This would have blocked out the sun, destroying much life on Earth.

Science and Technology

Scientists help us to figure out how things work. They ask questions and try to answer them by doing experiments. Scientists make very important discoveries. Without science we wouldn't have cars, TVs or mobile phones.

Technology

Have a look around the room you are in. Can you see anything that is made of plastic? Is there a clock? Or a window? All of these things were created with the help of science. Science has helped us invent tools and devices to make our lives easier. This is called technology.

Medicine

Hundreds of years ago even a fever could kill you. But in modern times we can make people better with antibiotic medicines. Antibiotics help our bodies to fight harmful germs. We also get shots or injections of medicines called vaccines when we are very young. They protect us from some diseases.

Computers

The first computers were so big they filled a whole room. Today, computers are more powerful and can fit into your schoolbag. Televisions, on the other hand, have become bigger and bigger.

▼ Laptop computers can be used anywhere, even when you're on a plane.

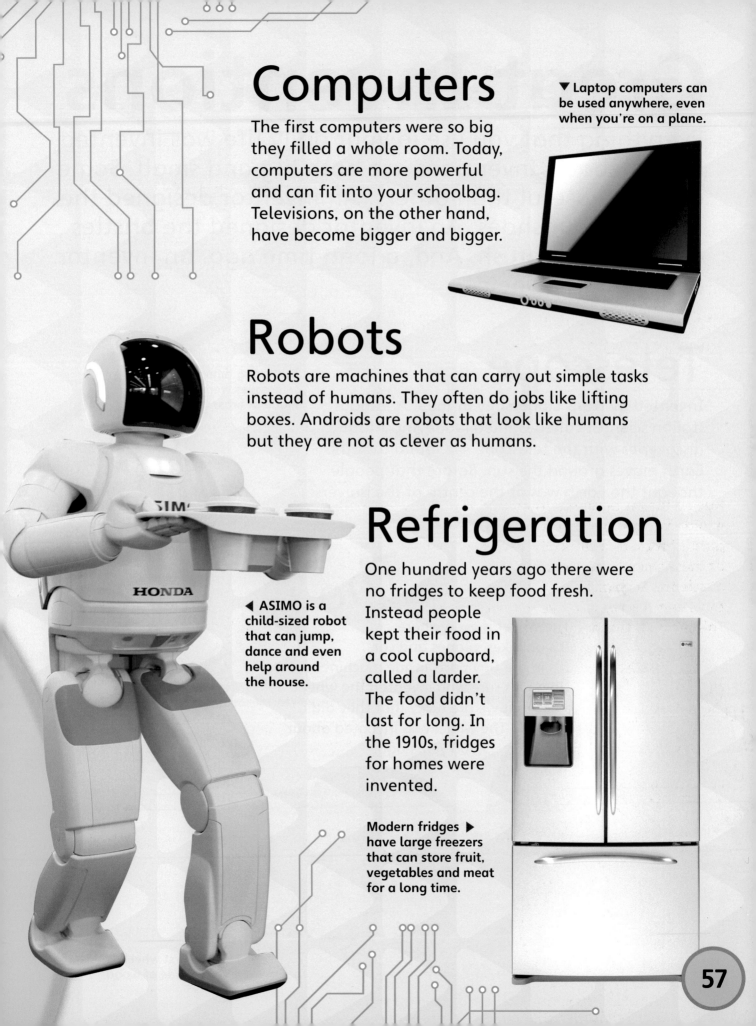

Robots

Robots are machines that can carry out simple tasks instead of humans. They often do jobs like lifting boxes. Androids are robots that look like humans but they are not as clever as humans.

◀ ASIMO is a child-sized robot that can jump, dance and even help around the house.

Refrigeration

One hundred years ago there were no fridges to keep food fresh. Instead people kept their food in a cool cupboard, called a larder. The food didn't last for long. In the 1910s, fridges for homes were invented.

Modern fridges ▶ have large freezers that can store fruit, vegetables and meat for a long time.

57

Great Inventions

Everything that you use in your daily life was invented by somebody. Inventions are both big and small. Some are more useful than others. An inventor designed the laces on your shoes. An inventor designed the bristles on your toothbrush. And, a long time ago, an inventor designed the wheel.

Telescope

Invented by Hans Lippershey in 1608. A famous Italian scientist called Galileo made important discoveries with the telescope. He found that the Earth moves around the sun. Before that people thought the Earth was at the centre of the universe.

For a long time, ▶ telescopes were made of brass.

The wheel is everywhere.
It's on bikes, planes and cars.
It's in the tiny parts inside machines.
No one is sure who invented the wheel,
but we are lucky that they did.
The wheel was invented about
5,000 years ago.

◀ The first wheels were made of wood.

Steam Engine

Invented by Thomas Savery in 1698. Early steam engines powered trains and ships. Steam was even used in the first cars. Wood or coal was burned to heat up water. Then the steam from the water would power the engine.

Steam locomotives ▼ were the first modern trains. They were launched in 1804.

Light Bulb

Invented by Humphry Davy in 1801. The first light bulbs only lasted a few minutes. In 1879 an inventor called Thomas Edison improved the design. He invented a light bulb that lasted for 40 hours.

Lens and shutter

Roll of film

Polaroid cameras ▶ were invented in 1947. They could produce prints almost instantly.

Camera

Invented by Joseph Nicéphore Niépce in the 1820s. Today, many people have a digital camera built into their mobile phone. In the 1800s, cameras were large wooden boxes. It took several hours to take one photograph.

Plastic

Invented by Alexander Parkes in 1855. Plastic is amazing because it can be moulded into so many shapes. Many of the objects around you are made from plastic. They include bottles, phones and pens.

Energy Everywhere

Energy is the power that makes everything work. The sun's energy keeps all living things alive on Earth. Electrical energy means we can light our homes at night. Without energy nothing would happen.

The Sun's Energy

Most of the energy in the world comes from the sun. Plants use energy from the sun to make food. Humans and animals eat plants and get energy too. We can use the sun's energy to do several things. We can use solar cookers to prepare food and solar collectors to heat water.

▼ The sun can also create other forms of energy. The sun shining on these solar panels is creating electricity.

Never Ending

Did you know that energy can never be used up? That is because energy never goes away—it just changes into another form of energy. There are two main types of energy.

1 Potential Energy

Potential energy is energy that is stored up. A slingshot bungee is a ride that shoots you into the air with large elastic ropes. As the ropes are pulled tight, they store potential energy.

2 Kinetic Energy

When something is moving it is using kinetic energy. When the bungee ropes are released, the stored energy turns into kinetic energy. The bungee jumper is shot high up into the air.

Electricity

Electricity is the main source of energy for us. We create electricity using flowing water, wind, waves, and the sun. Electricity is stored at power stations. It is then sent out through power lines to our homes.

Nuclear power plants ▶ generate electricity by splitting uranium atoms.

61

History of Communication

When we communicate we share information and ideas with other people. There are many different ways to communicate. We send each other text messages and e-mails. We call each other on the phone or meet to talk. We watch television, listen to the radio and read books and newspapers.

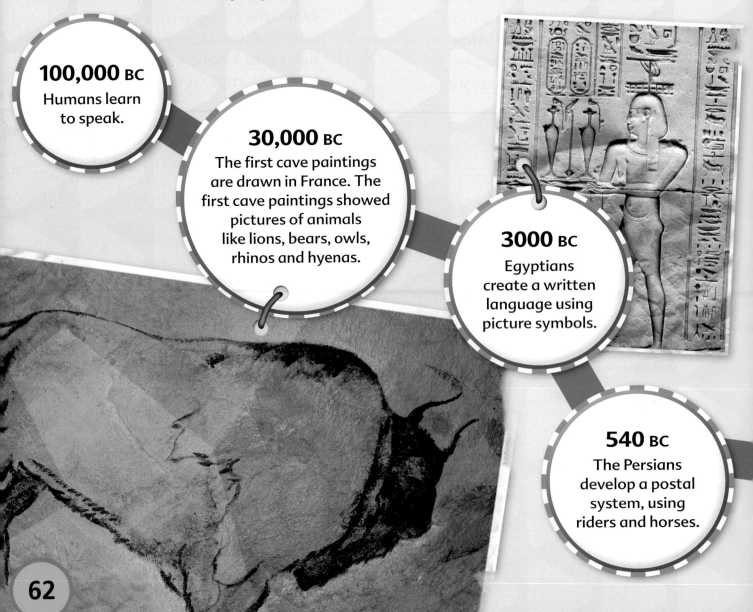

100,000 BC
Humans learn to speak.

30,000 BC
The first cave paintings are drawn in France. The first cave paintings showed pictures of animals like lions, bears, owls, rhinos and hyenas.

3000 BC
Egyptians create a written language using picture symbols.

540 BC
The Persians develop a postal system, using riders and horses.

1994
The Internet becomes popular in homes.

1973
The first mobile phone is shown to the world. It weighed as much as a pineapple and cost over £2,000 to buy.

1940–1945
The first modern computers are developed. One of the early computers was the ENIAC, built in 1946. The computer was called the 'giant brain.' It was so big it filled up a whole room.

1935
The first regular television broadcasts are made in Germany.

1901
Radio is broadcast across the Atlantic Ocean for the first time.

1209 AD
Mongolian warlord Genghis Khan uses pigeons to send messages. The message would simply be attached to a pigeon, which would then fly home with it.

1450
The modern printing press is invented. Now books and newspapers can be easily printed.

1876
Alexander Graham Bell invents the first telephone.

Your Body

The human body is an amazing living machine. It tells you when you are hungry and when you need to sleep. Your body helps you in every way it can. You must keep your body healthy and fit.

What is the Body Made of?

Your body is made of many tiny cells. Different types of cells stick to each other to create your body parts. Your little toe alone is made of around two billion cells.

This is a picture of bone cells under ▶ a microscope. Each ball is one cell.

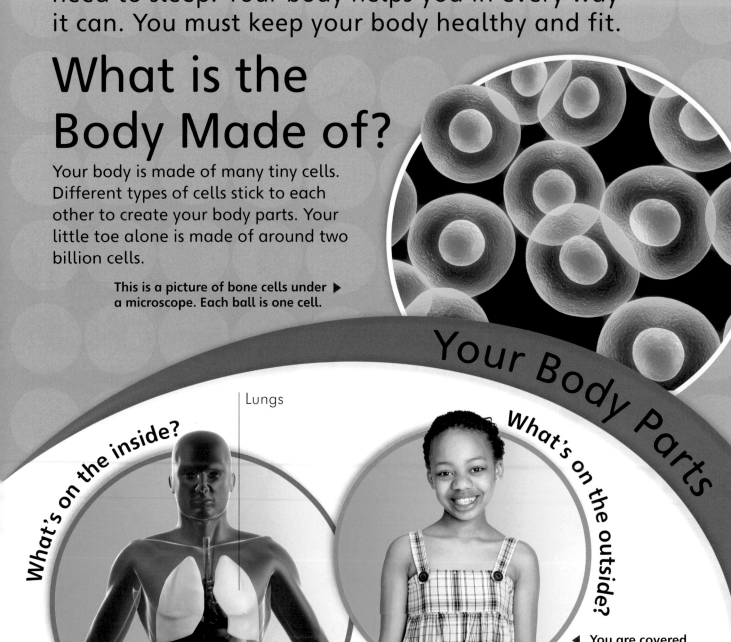

Your Body Parts

Lungs

What's on the inside?

What's on the outside?

Intestines

Liver   Heart

◀ Organs are special parts inside your body. Each organ does an important job to keep your body working.

◀ You are covered from head to toe in skin. It is your body's largest organ! Your skin is a protective layer for you organs and tissues. It also releases sweat to cool you down.

Staying Healthy

You can help your body work well by staying healthy. This means exercising and eating the right food. Running, dancing and playing sports are good ways to exercise. Fruit and vegetables are very healthy foods.

Eat a 'rainbow' of ▶ fruit and vegetables. Different colours contain unique nutrients.

Many Colours

The colour of your skin is affected by a substance called melanin. People with dark skin have more melanin and people with light skin have less.

◀ People from hot countries often have dark skin. Darker skin does not get sunburnt easily.

Only You

Did you know that four humans are born every second? But every one of them is different. So are you. There is nobody else that looks, acts or thinks exactly like you.

All of us our born with ▶ certain characteristics that we get from both parents.

65

Heart, Lungs and Blood

Your heart, lungs and blood make sure you get enough oxygen to live. Your lungs breathe in air. Your blood takes oxygen to different parts of your body. Your heart pumps out clean blood.

Heart

Your heart is a powerful organ that is always working. It receives and pumps out blood to the entire body. The movement of blood through the heart causes the heart muscles to expand and contract. This is called the heartbeat. Your heart beats between 70 and 140 times a minute.

▼ **This is what an adult heart looks like.**

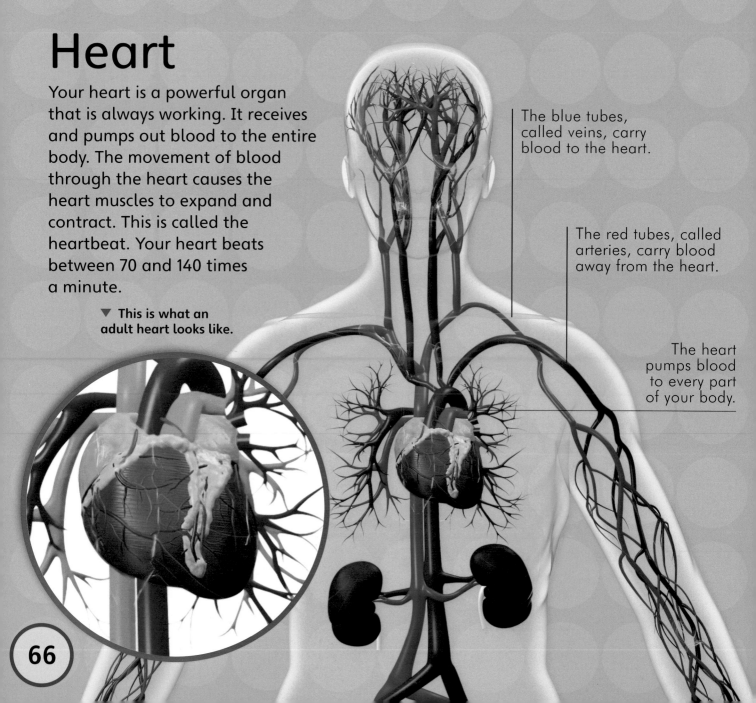

The blue tubes, called veins, carry blood to the heart.

The red tubes, called arteries, carry blood away from the heart.

The heart pumps blood to every part of your body.

Blood is the most important fluid produced by our body. It keeps us alive. Blood transports oxygen to the different parts of our body. It travels through tubes called blood vessels.

There are three different types of cells in blood.

Platelets

Platelets (tiny ▶ parts of a blood cell) prevent us from bleeding too much when we get hurt.

Red blood cells ▼ carry oxygen.

White blood cells

White blood ▶ cells help us fight disease.

Red blood cells

Lungs

When we breathe we suck air into our lungs. Our lungs send the oxygen from the air into our blood. We breathe out carbon dioxide, which we don't need. Air is the fuel that keeps us alive. Without it we would die.

▼ When you breathe in, your lungs fill with air and your ribs move outwards. A muscle under your ribs called the diaphragm helps you to breathe.

Air goes in

Lungs fill with air

Ribs move outwards

Diaphragm rises

Carbon dioxide goes out

Lungs empty out air

Ribs move inwards

Diaphragm goes flat

67

Muscles and Bones

Your bones and muscles are what keep you upright and let you move. Without bones your body would fall in a heap. Without muscles you would not be able to dance, smile or poke out your tongue.

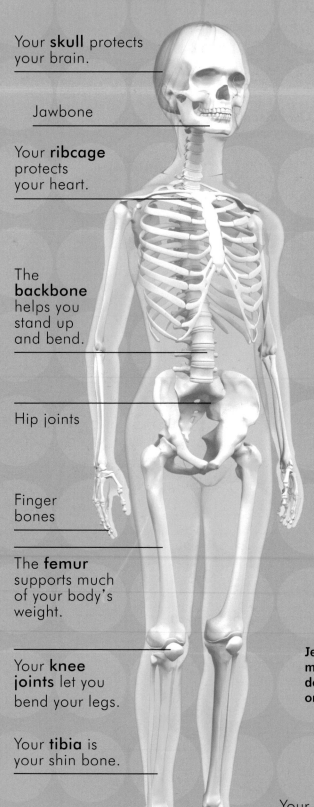

Your **skull** protects your brain.

Jawbone

Your **ribcage** protects your heart.

The **backbone** helps you stand up and bend.

Hip joints

Finger bones

The **femur** supports much of your body's weight.

Your **knee joints** let you bend your legs.

Your **tibia** is your shin bone.

Your **feet bones** make up a quarter of your bones.

The Skeleton

Your skeleton is a framework of bones. There are 206 bones in an adult's skeleton. Your skeleton gives your body its shape. It also protects the soft organs inside, like your heart.

◀ Bones are made of calcium and other hard minerals.

No Skeleton?

A jellyfish is one of many animals without a skeleton. It is supported by the sea. But if the jellyfish were on land it would collapse.

Jellyfish are made ▶ mostly of water. They don't have a heart or brain.

Muscles

Your muscles cover your skeleton. They are attached to the bones. When you move, your muscles pull the bone. This moves you into different positions. Your biggest muscle is the gluteus maximus. It forms most of your bottom.

Bones

Human bones are hard, light and tough. Bones are also alive. They grow and can fix themselves if they break. Bones store important minerals and vitamins. They also produce red blood cells.

Your thigh bone is the ▶ longest and thickest bone in your body. It is called a femur.

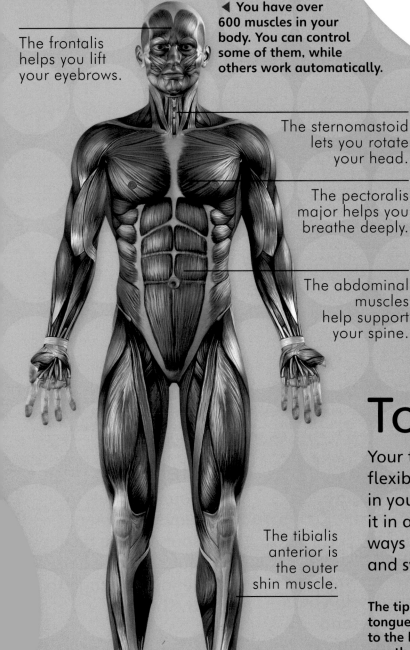

◀ You have over 600 muscles in your body. You can control some of them, while others work automatically.

The frontalis helps you lift your eyebrows.

The sternomastoid lets you rotate your head.

The pectoralis major helps you breathe deeply.

The abdominal muscles help support your spine.

The tibialis anterior is the outer shin muscle.

There are 20 muscles in each foot.

Always Working

Some muscles work automatically to protect you and keep you alive. Muscles around your eyes blink to stop your eyes from drying out. The heart muscles make sure it is always beating.

Tongue

Your tongue is the most flexible set of muscles in your body. You move it in all sorts of strange ways to talk, eat and swallow.

The tip of your ▶ tongue pushes food to the back of your mouth so you can chew it properly.

Senses and the Brain

The brain is the most complex organ of the body. It has billions of tiny cells that work to make sense of the world around you. The brain is why we can think, feel, see, taste, touch, smell and hear.

Senses

Your body sends information to your brain about what is going on around you. It does this through your five senses—smell, taste, sight, hearing and touch.

Touching
Our skin has millions of nerves. When we touch something, these nerves tell us what it feels like.

Seeing
Your eyes are like cameras in your head. They tell the brain what they are seeing.

Tasting
Your tongue has tiny little bumps on it that let you taste. These are called taste buds.

Smelling
Nerves in your nose help you understand what you are smelling.

Hearing
Sound travels in waves. When a sound wave reaches our ears, the ears send a message to the brain.

Brain

Your brain is the control centre of your body. It tells your body what to do. In return your body tells your brain what is happening to it. Your brain is how you think and make decisions. Your brain is working while you are awake and even while you are asleep.

▼ **Your brain is made up of parts that carry out different tasks.**

Parietal lobe (processing sensory information)

Frontal lobe (planning, problem-solving)

Temporal lobe (language, learning)

Occipital lobe (visual perception)

Cerebellum (balance)

Brain stem (regulates heart rate, breathing)

◄ Sneezing is a reflex action.

Nerves

Your brain sends and receives messages through nerves. Nerves are thin fibres that run all around your body.

The brain and spinal ▶ **cord make up the Central Nervous System (CNS). All nerves are connected to the CNS.**

Brain

Spinal cord

Reflex Actions

Most of the time we tell our body what to do, such as standing up. But sometimes the body makes a sudden movement, like pulling away from something hot. This is called a reflex action.

Transport and Travel

People need to move themselves or their things from one place to another. Long ago, people used boats or carts pulled by horses to travel. Today, we use fast machines like cars, aeroplanes and trains. Let's first look at some unusual ways to travel.

Segway

People ride this two-wheel vehicle standing up. The rider leans forward or backwards to move. It has an engine powered by a battery.

Handlebar with a speed-limiting mechanism.

Tourists use Segways ▲ for sightseeing and theme park rides.

Base

Wheels

Have You Tried This?

▲ A good launch and wind can make the glider reach a speed of 145 km per hour.

Hang glider

A hang glider is a type of light aircraft for one person. Hang gliders have no engine. Instead they are launched off a hill or cliff. The rider is attached to the cross bar.

72

Spaceplane

A spaceplane is a type of aircraft that can take passengers into space. It travels for about two hours and can carry up to eight people. It is very expensive to buy a ticket.

White Knight II

The spaceplane SpaceShipOne is ▶ carried almost 17 km into the air by its mothership White Knight II and later blasted into space.

SpaceShipOne

Carrier engine

Rocket engine

Carrier wings

Foldable wings

Sled

A sled is a vehicle that is pulled by horses or dogs across snow and ice. It has rails beneath it to make it slide. It was one of the first forms of transportation.

Kayak

This light boat is hollow so a person can sit inside. It is powered with a paddle. Inuit people have used kayaks for years to fish and hunt in cold Arctic waters.

Boot space to keep hunting gear

People use kayaks ▶ to go fishing or take pictures of water animals.

Double-bladed paddle

On Land

There are many different forms of transport on land. Trucks, buses, cars and motorbikes can travel fast on roads. Bikes are slower, but you can get around on them, too. Trains move at high speeds along railway tracks.

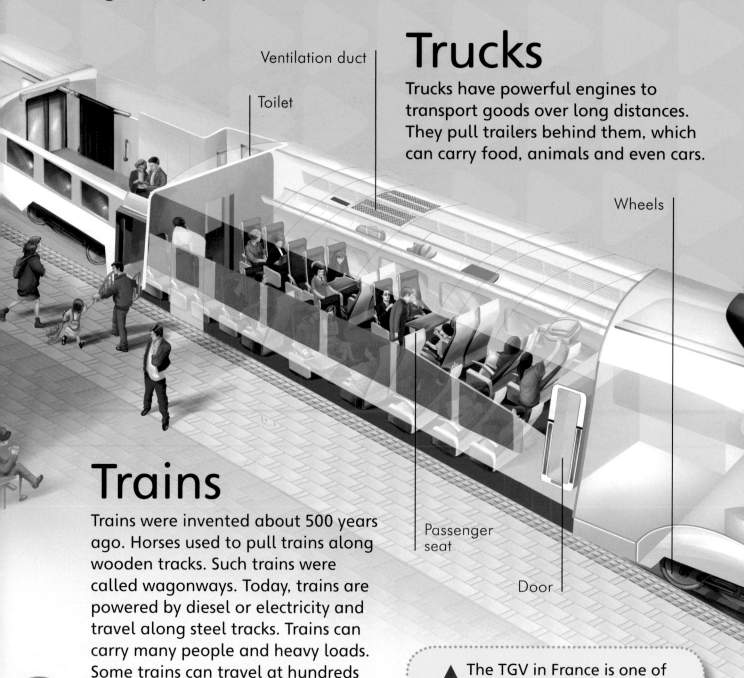

Ventilation duct

Toilet

Trucks

Trucks have powerful engines to transport goods over long distances. They pull trailers behind them, which can carry food, animals and even cars.

Wheels

Trains

Trains were invented about 500 years ago. Horses used to pull trains along wooden tracks. Such trains were called wagonways. Today, trains are powered by diesel or electricity and travel along steel tracks. Trains can carry many people and heavy loads. Some trains can travel at hundreds of kilometres or miles an hour.

Passenger seat

Door

▲ The TGV in France is one of the world's fastest trains. It can reach 570 km an hour.

Bikes

Bicycles are two-wheeled machines usually ridden by one person. Bicycles do not need petrol. A rider turns the bicycle wheels by pushing on the pedals. Bicycles are quiet and good for the environment. Motorbikes are fast, loud and have a petrol engine.

▲ **Some racing motorbikes are known to reach a speed of 564 km per hour.**

Controls

Driver

Tracks

Engine

Cars

There are about a billion cars in the world. Cars have four wheels and a petrol or diesel engine but more and more cars are being powered by electricity. This is much better for the environment.

Cars are the most recycled ▼ consumer product in the world.

Double-decker bus ▶ is a common way to get around London.

Buses

Buses are designed to transport many people at once. Buses are often used as public transport. They carry people to work or school, or from place to place in a city. Buses also travel long distances between towns.

75

On Water

Boats carry people and goods across water. They have been used since ancient times. Early boats were small and used sails and oars to move. Later, propellers were invented to power big ships. Today, rivers, lakes and oceans are full of different types of boats and ships.

Cruise Ships

Cruise ships are designed to take people on ocean holidays. The larger ones can carry thousands of passengers. On board the ship are restaurants, shops, swimming pools, basketball courts, cinemas and gardens.

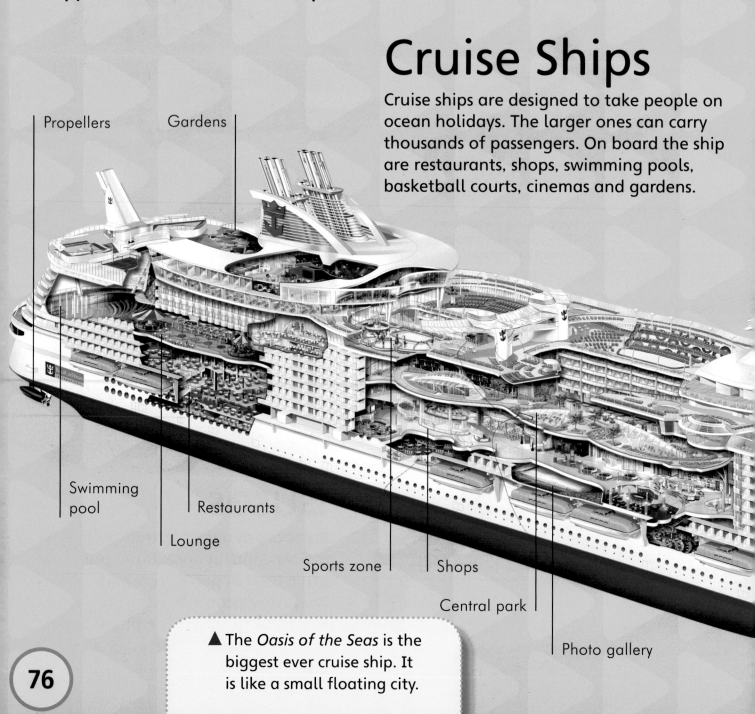

Propellers

Gardens

Swimming pool

Restaurants

Lounge

Sports zone

Shops

Central park

Photo gallery

▲ The *Oasis of the Seas* is the biggest ever cruise ship. It is like a small floating city.

Supertankers

Container ships and supertankers are massive ships that transport goods. Supertankers carry oil across the oceans. They are the largest ships in the world. Small tugboats are needed to guide the supertankers into port.

Supertankers can carry ▶ millions of barrels of oil.

Hovercraft

A hovercraft travels over the water on a cushion of air. They are also called air-cushion vehicles (ACVs). Hovercrafts often carry passengers on short sea journeys. They use large propellers to move them forward.

▼ Hovercrafts can travel over land as well as water.

Submarine

Not all boats travel on the surface of the water. Submarines can dive beneath the waves. They can explore the bottom of the ocean.

Submarines are designed ▼ to stay underwater for months at a time.

Cabins

Golf course

Helipad

Cinema

In the Air

People have always dreamed of flying like birds. This dream came true over 100 years ago when aeroplanes were invented. Now, aeroplanes are a common way of travelling long distances quickly. Thousands of people travel by air every day.

Aeroplane

Orville Wright was the first person to fly a plane, in 1903. Only one person could fit into his plane. Today, jumbo jets can carry over 800 passengers. The biggest aeroplanes are designed to carry heavy loads. They can even carry other aircraft.

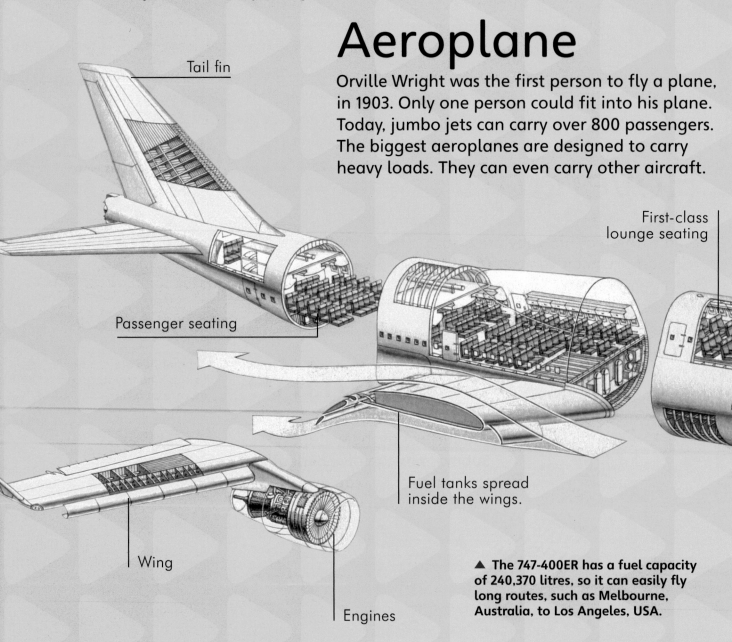

Tail fin

First-class lounge seating

Passenger seating

Fuel tanks spread inside the wings.

Wing

Engines

▲ The 747-400ER has a fuel capacity of 240,370 litres, so it can easily fly long routes, such as Melbourne, Australia, to Los Angeles, USA.

▲ The Boeing 747 has a hump-like upperdeck, for extra seating or as a cargo carrier.

Helicopter

A helicopter has blades instead of wings. The blades spin around very fast to lift the helicopter. Helicopters can fly up, down, backwards, forwards and sideways. They can even hover in the air.

▲ A helicopter has blades at the top to lift it. It has blades at the back to keep it stable.

Hot-air balloon

A hot-air balloon gets its power from hot gas. The gas heats up the air in the balloon, which makes it float up. Passengers ride in a basket underneath the balloon.

◀ The first flight in a hot-air balloon took place in 1783.

Flight deck

Flight Mechanism

The flow of air ▼ across the wings of birds.

Reduced air pressure

Constant air pressure

How do Planes Fly?

Planes can fly because of the shape of their wings. They are curved on the top and flat underneath. As air flows over the wing it lifts it up. Bird wings are also shaped this way.

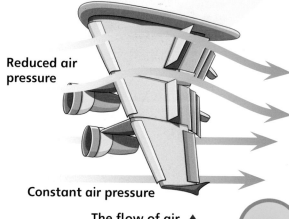

Reduced air pressure

Constant air pressure

The flow of air ▲ across plane wings.

Human History

The first humans led simple lives hunting and gathering. They moved from place to place to find food and developed tools to help them hunt. We know about the first humans from the tools, pots and paintings they left behind.

Hunters and Gatherers

Early people ate basic food. They hunted animals such as pigs, deer and horses. They also gathered nuts, roots, berries and insects. People would move if food ran out or the weather became cold. They slept in caves or made tents from leaves, branches and animal skins.

Bones, paintings and tools dating back thousands ▶ of years have been found in caves all over the world.

▼ People used fire for warmth, light and cooking as far back as 400,000 years ago.

Villages

Over time, people became successful farmers and had more than enough to eat. This gave them more time to do other things. They made clay pots, clothes from wool, and built bigger houses. Groups of houses became villages.

Pottery was one of the first ▶ crafts developed by humans.

Farmers

Around 10,000 years ago people began to settle in one place. They grew their own crops, like wheat and barley. They also learned to keep sheep and goats for their meat and milk. These people were the first farmers.

◀ Hammers were among the earliest tools.

Towns and Cities

As villages became bigger they grew into towns. Towns had all the things people needed in one place. A town might have had shops, houses, a church, a doctor and a wall to protect it. Many years later, larger towns turned into cities. These became the cities that we live in today.

▼ London, the capital of England, was established as a city more than 2,000 years ago.

81

Ancient Egyptians

The ancient Egyptians lived thousands of years ago by the banks of the River Nile. Here they built amazing temples, pyramids and cities. They worshipped many gods and were ruled over by a king called a pharaoh.

Nile Flood

The first Egyptians were farmers. They grew crops and raised animals by the River Nile. Every year the river would flood, bringing with it rich, black mud. This mud was perfect for growing crops.

Ancient Egyptian paintings show ▶ farmers busy at work in their fields.

Pharaoh

The pharaoh was the most powerful person in ancient Egypt. Pharaohs were looked after by many servants and lived a life of luxury. People believed the pharaoh was a living god. Huge statues would be built of the pharaoh, such as Ramesses II.

The temple of Abu Simbel features ▶ four giant statues of Ramesses II.

Pyramids

Pyramids were enormous stone tombs that took many years to build. The pharaoh would be buried in the pyramid after he died. The pharaoh's treasures, food, boats and furniture would be buried with him. Pyramids were often built like mazes inside to stop robbers stealing the treasures.

▼ The pyramids were built out of huge blocks of stone, especially limestone.

Mummies

The Egyptians believed a person would go to a new world after they died. So, they mummified the body to keep it in good condition. This meant drying the body out by embalming it and wrapping it in bandages. It would then be placed in a special coffin called a sarcophagus.

The golden sarcophagus ▶ of King Tutankhamun, who ruled Egypt more than 3,500 years ago.

Ancient Greeks

Ancient Greece was not one country ruled over by a king. Instead it was made up of several different cities. These cities would sometimes join together to fight the enemies of Greece. The most powerful city was called Athens.

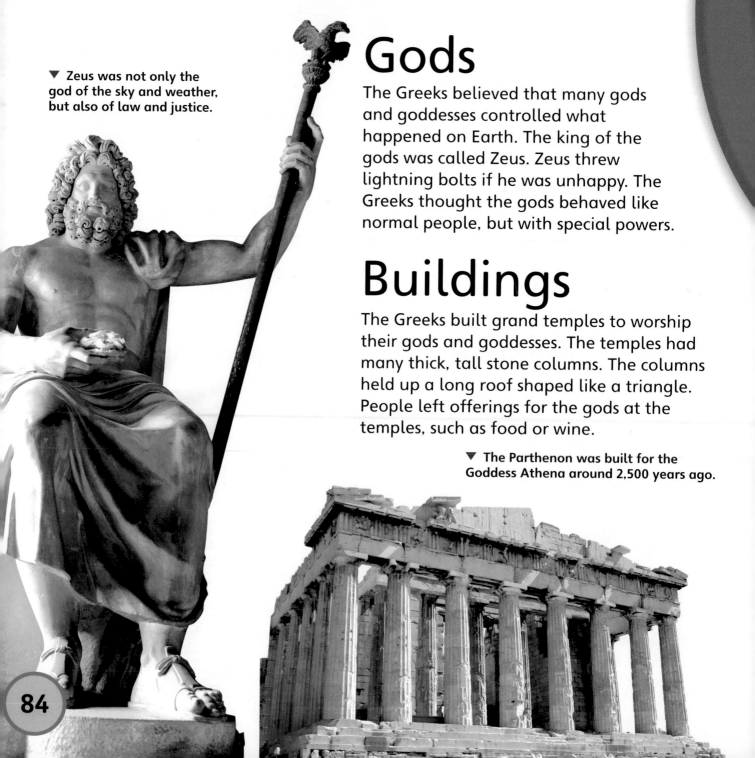

▼ Zeus was not only the god of the sky and weather, but also of law and justice.

Gods

The Greeks believed that many gods and goddesses controlled what happened on Earth. The king of the gods was called Zeus. Zeus threw lightning bolts if he was unhappy. The Greeks thought the gods behaved like normal people, but with special powers.

Buildings

The Greeks built grand temples to worship their gods and goddesses. The temples had many thick, tall stone columns. The columns held up a long roof shaped like a triangle. People left offerings for the gods at the temples, such as food or wine.

▼ The Parthenon was built for the Goddess Athena around 2,500 years ago.

The Greeks loved to compete at sports. Their sports included running, jumping, boxing and wrestling. The Greeks started the Olympic Games, which is still held today. In ancient Greece, though, only men could participate in the events.

▼ Many athletes in ancient Greece did not wear clothes during sporting events.

The Olympic Games

Plays

The first plays were first written and performed in Greece. Only men were allowed to act. They had to act the parts of women and men. They used masks to show if they were angry, happy or sad.

Soldiers

Each city had its own army and navy. The best soldiers were from a city called Sparta. They were very tough. Spartan soldiers were trained to live in the freezing cold and go without food and water.

Statue of the Spartan warrior-king Leonidas I, ▶ famous for his bravery on the battlefield.

Ancient Rome

Rome began as a small settlement 2,000 years ago, yet it grew into one of the mightiest empires of the ancient world. The Roman Empire ruled over most of modern-day Europe. The Romans invented many things we still use today.

Rome

Rome was once the most important city in the world. People from all around the world lived in Rome. It contained hundreds of buildings, including temples, bathhouses and apartments. Many ancient Roman buildings are still standing today.

Aqueducts

The Romans invented a way of controlling water, called aqueducts. Aqueducts were long channels stretching for many kilometres. They would bring clean water into the city, while sewers took dirty water out. We use a similar system in modern cities.

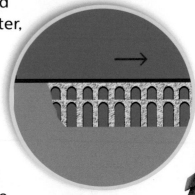

▲ Most Roman aqueducts were constructed from granite blocks, without using mortar.

◀ The Colosseum was a grand open-air theatre that could seat up to 50,000 people.

Baths

The Romans built public baths in every one of their cities. Inside the baths were rooms with hot steam and cold pools. People would clean themselves with olive oil instead of soap. Almost everyone would visit the baths regularly to get clean and relax.

◀ An old Roman bath still exists in Bath, England.

Gladiators

Gladiators were men who were forced to fight each other. Sometimes they also had to fight wild animals, such as lions and elephants. Gladiators sometimes died during these fights. Romans went to see gladiators fight in a huge building called the Colosseum.

Army

The Roman Empire had the greatest army of the ancient world. The soldiers were well trained and clever in battle. The army invaded many new countries. The countries would then become part of the empire. The army also built roads across the empire.

▲ Augustus was the first emperor of the Roman Empire. He ruled for about 41 years.

The Vikings

The Vikings were a proud warrior race that came from Norway, Sweden and Denmark. Around 1,000 years ago, the Vikings would make long voyages to distant lands. When they landed they would either trade with foreign villages, settle in them or attack them.

Longboats

Viking longboats were built to travel huge distances through rough seas. Vikings would often be stuck in longboats for weeks at a time. Longboats used both sails and oars. This meant they could move very fast in the water.

▼ The head of a serpent or dragon was often carved onto longboats to scare off sea monsters.

Crafts

The Vikings made many beautiful necklaces, armbands and brooches from gold, silver and glass. They used animal horns for cups and made combs from bone. Men wore little leather pouches to hold their eating knives.

▲ This gold ring from the 10th century is an example of Viking craftsmanship.

Viking Homes

Viking houses were called longhouses. They were often made from wood or stone. Inside there was one long room where everyone, including barn animals, lived. A fire in the middle of the longhouse kept it warm.

▼ A hole in the roof took out the smoke from the longhouse's fireplace

Warrior Wear

Viking warriors wore padded clothes and shoes made from wool and animal skin. They would wear chain mail armour over their clothes. They would also wear a helmet with a nose guard.

◀ Warriors always carried a spear and a large knife called a *seax*. They also used swords and axes.

The Middle Ages

The Middle Ages (5th to 15th centuries) were a time of kings, knights and castles. In Europe, many battles were fought over who owned land. Kings and lords would protect themselves and their people behind strong castle walls.

Living in Castles

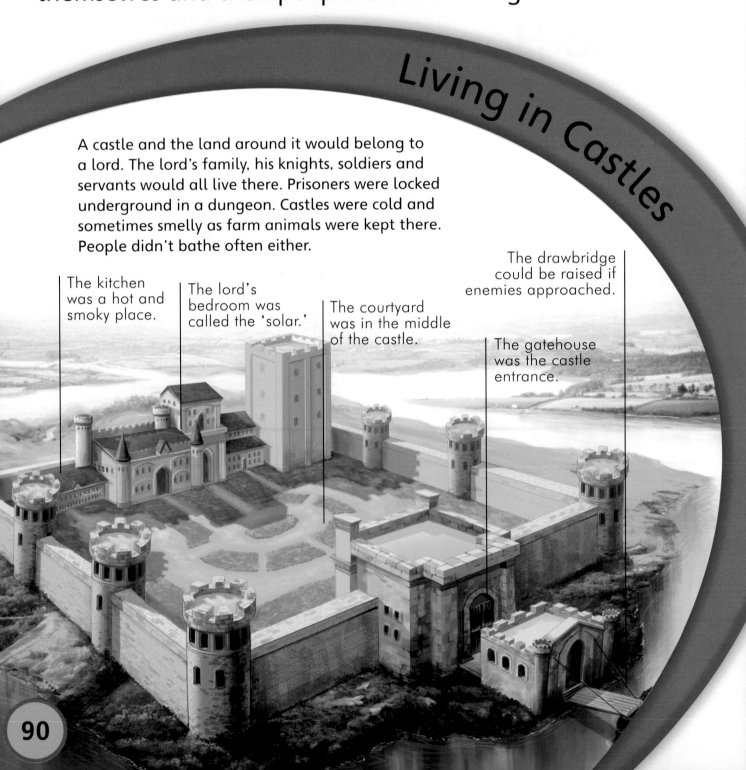

A castle and the land around it would belong to a lord. The lord's family, his knights, soldiers and servants would all live there. Prisoners were locked underground in a dungeon. Castles were cold and sometimes smelly as farm animals were kept there. People didn't bathe often either.

The kitchen was a hot and smoky place.

The lord's bedroom was called the 'solar.'

The courtyard was in the middle of the castle.

The drawbridge could be raised if enemies approached.

The gatehouse was the castle entrance.

Banquets

A banquet was a huge feast held in the castle's great hall. Guests enjoyed many meats, pies, puddings and ales. Musicians and a jester would entertain everyone.

Peasants

Peasants or farmers had a tough life during the Middle Ages. They worked in the lord's fields looking after the crops. The peasants had to make sure there was enough food for the castle. They also had to fight for the lord if asked to do so.

Knights

Knights were nobles who fought for their lord or king. A young boy could train to become a knight. First he would serve at a castle as a page. Then he would become a squire and learn to use weapons. Finally, the king or lord of the castle would make him a knight.

◀ **Knights held contests, called jousts, in which they used their lances to knock each other off their horses.**

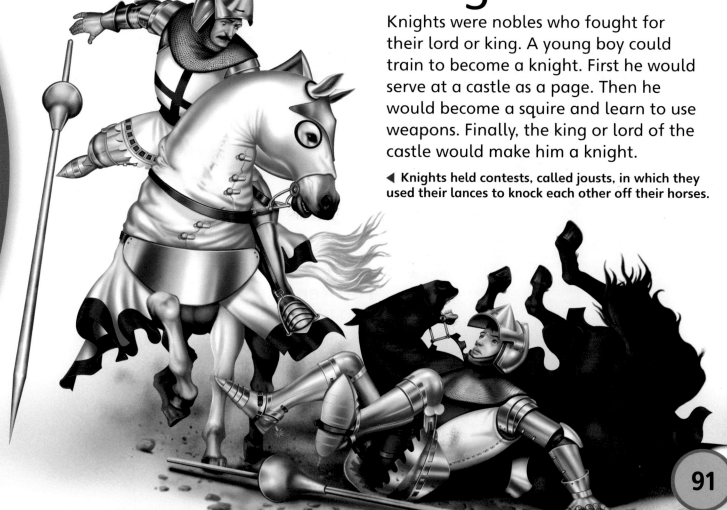

91

The Modern World

There have been many changes since the Middle Ages. These changes have shaped the way people live today. During this time faraway lands were discovered, new machines invented, and world wars fought. Humans have even travelled into space.

Revolutions
(18th century)

There were several revolutions in modern times. Between 1775 and 1783 in America, the people went to war with their British rulers and threw them out. They then formed a new country, now known as the United States of America.

The Age of Discovery
(15th to 17th centuries)

During this time, European explorers sailed the seas looking for goods, riches and new lands. Europeans visited Africa, Asia, Australasia and the Americas for the first time. An Italian called Christopher Columbus discovered North America.

The Renaissance
(Europe: 14th to 17th centuries)

This was an important period for art, science and inventions. Leonardo da Vinci painted one of the most famous pictures ever, the *Mona Lisa*. He also made discoveries about how the body works.

The Industrial Age
(Britain: 18th to 19th centuries)

This was a time when new machines were invented and used to make goods in large, smoky factories. Many people moved to cities to work in factories. Poor children also had to work. Conditions in the cities and factories were bad. Many people became sick and died.

World Wars
(20th century)

In the 20th century there were two terrible world wars. World War I lasted from 1914 to 1918, and World War II from 1939 to 1945. Millions of people were killed and dozens of cities were destroyed.

Space Age
(20th century)

In 1961, a Russian named Yuri Gagarin became the first man to travel into space. In 1969, an American called Neil Armstrong was the first man to walk on the moon.

City Living
(20th to 21st centuries)

Over the last 100 years many people have moved from the countryside into the cities. People often move to a city to find better work. Around half of the world's people now live in a city.

Index

94

Picture Credits

Front Cover:
© Shutterstock.com: Oleksiy Mark

Half title:
© Shutterstock.com: Oleksiy Mark

Full title:
© Shutterstock.com: Oleksiy Mark

Content Page:
Shutterstock: Cloki; Dokoupilova; Dennis Donohue; Karina Wallton; Sculpies
NASA: Goddard Space Flight Center Scientific Visualization Studio
Photolibrary: Jupiterimages

Agustawestland: 79(t)
American Honda Motor Co., Inc.: 57(bl)
Antarctic Photo Library: Robyn Waserman/National Science Foundation 49(bl); Paul Thur/National Science Foundation/Antarctic Photo Library
BibleWalks.com—Holy Land Biblical sites review: 80
Bigstock: Paul fleet 47(b)
Centers for Disease Control and Prevention: Dr. Mae Melvin 67(tr)
Dreamstime: Sebastian Kaulitzki 18(c); Hugoht 29(c); Stefan Baum 30; Maksym Gorpenyuk 34(b); Tracey Taylor 46(t); Jasna 46(b); Wong Hock Weng John 52(bl); Kandasamy M 69(tr); Brancaleone 87(b)
ESO: Yuri Beletsky 8(br)
Getty Images: Stephen Biesty/Getty Images 78-79; Viking/The Bridgeman Art Library 89(tl)
General Electric Company 1997-2010: 57(br)
Istockphoto: Btrenkel 31(t); Jani Bryson 65(c); Jean Morin 81(tr)
Judy Patrick: 77(c)
Mercedes-Benz: 75(tr)
NASA: ESA/The Hubble SM4 ERO 7(b); JPL-Caltech 6-7; JPL 10-11; 12; 13; 12-13; 14(tr); JPL 14(cr); Goddard Space Flight Center Scientific Visualization Studio 15(c); 14-15; Goddard Space Flight Center Scientific Visualization Studio 25(t); 27(l); JPL-Caltech 80(b); 93(t)
National Science Foundation: Henry Kaiser 68-69(c)
Nellis.af.mil: 60
Photolibrary: Jeffrey L. Rotman 18(b); Jupiterimages 31(c); Dan Porges 33(b); Heinz Plenge 41(b); 63(c); 3LH-B&W 63(bl);

Marcia Hartsock/The Medical File 71(tr); Dea/G Sioen 82(c); Robert Harding(b); Tyler Olson 89(cr); Barrett & MacKay 89(bl); The Print Collector 92
Rex Features: Nils Jorgensen 59(tr)
Shutterstock: Prima 10; Samuel Acosta 14(cr); Matthew Cole 14(b); JuliusKielaitis 16; James M Phelps, Jr 17(t); Keith Levit 17(b); Beboy 21; Costazzurra 23(tr); Lafoto 23(bl); Chee-Onn Leong 23(br); Pichugin Dmitry 24(tl); Elenamiv 24(tr); Kai Wong 24(bl); Rob Huntley 24(br); Prima 25(b); JeremyRichards 26; Cloki 27(r); Henryk Sadura 28; Puchan 29(t); Mike Flippo 31(b); Jaimaa 32; Ayazad 33(t); Akva 33(c); Subbotina Anna 34; Julius Elias 34(c); Pius Lee 35(t); 36-37; Jeroen Beerten 38; Dokoupilova 39(tr); WDG Photo 39(br); Gert Johannes Jacobus Very 38-39; Karen Givens 40; Ncn 41(c); Palko 42; Eric Isselee 43(t); Jason Prince 43(b); Miki Verebes 42-43; Tezzstock 44; Fivespots 45(t); Matthew Cole 45(c); Marie C Fields 45(br); Lavigne herve 47(c); Peter Kirillov 48; Similaun Man 49(br); Cheryl E. Davis 51(t); Steve Byland 51(c); James Steidl 51(b); Dennis Donohue 50-51; Andre Goncalves 52(c); Julien 53(c); Palko 53(br); Monkey Business Images 56; ArchMan 57(t); James Steidl 58; Tr3gin 59(cr); Karina Wallton 59(bl); David Adamson 61(t); Martin Murnsky 61(b); Haridehal Abhirama Ashwin 62(cr); Awe Inspiring Images 62(bl); Sebastian Kaulitzki 64(cr), 64(bl); Yuri Arcurs 64(br); Hannamariah 65(t); Joshhhab 65(b); Sebastian Kaulitzki 66; Deaff 67(cl); Sebastian Kaulitzki 68; Sebastian Kaulitzki 69(l); Lana K 69(br); Liudmila P. Sundikova 70; Yakobchuk Vasyl 71(cl); Mandy Godbehear 71(bl); Peter Wey 73(tr); Stephen Bonk 73(b); Julie Lucht 75(tl); Jose Gill 77(t); Andrea Danti 77(br); Samuel Acosta 79(c); Hvoya 79(b); Sergey Kamshylin 81(tr); Fcarucci 81(b); Anthon Jackson 83(t); Sculpies 82-83; Kasa.dome 84(bl); Andrey Grinyov 84(br); Natalia Pavlova 85; Samot 86; Chad Bontrager 87(t); Emin kuliyev 93(b)
Science Photo Library: Pekka Parviainen
Segway Inc.: 72(tr)
U.S. Navy: Terry Matlock 19; Lt. Cmdr. Brian Riley 23(tl)
US Army: 63(t)
Virgingalactic: Jim Koepnick 73(tr)

Q2AMedia Art Bank: Content Page; 15; 18-19; 20-21; 22; 25; 26-27; 28-29; 39; 40-41; 50; 52-53; 54-55; 56-57; 58-59; 67; 74-75; 76-77; 85; 86-87; 88; 90-91